Zero to Hero
Unlocking Creativity with Generative AI

By Evan Parker

Harness AI to transform your creativity into success!

First Edition

Published by Self-Published
2024

Copyright © 2024 by Evan Parker
All rights reserved. No part of this book may be reproduced, stored in a retrieval system, or transmitted in any form or by any means—electronic, mechanical, photocopying, recording, or otherwise—without prior permission of the author.

For the dreamers who dare to create.

Zero to Hero: Unlocking Creativity with AI

Chapter 1: Your Hero's Journey with Generative AI 1

Chapter 2. Discovering Generative AI: The Tools of the Trade 13

Chapter 3: Turning Ideas into Action 25

Chapter 4: Mastering the Art of Prompts 33

Chapter 5: Overcoming Creative Blocks with AI 46

Chapter 6: Refining and Polishing: The AI Advantage . 57

Chapter 7: Scaling Your Efforts: Beyond the First Creation 69

Chapter 8: The Ethics of AI in Creativity 81

Chapter 9: Building Personal and Professional Branding with AI 94

Chapter 10: From Passion to Profession: Launching Your AI-Powered Business 106

Chapter 11: Generative AI in Education and Learning 119

Chapter 12: The Future of Storytelling with AI 132

Chapter 13: Creating for the Metaverse 144

Chapter 14: Monetizing Creativity: Proven Strategies for Success 156

Zero to Hero: Unlocking Creativity with AI

Chapter 15: AI and Sustainability: Innovating for a Better World 169

Chapter 16: Collaborative Creativity: Teaming Up with AI and Humans 182

Chapter 17: Monetizing Niche Opportunities with AI 193

Chapter 18: Gamifying Your Creative Journey 205

Chapter 19: AI and Hyper-Personalization 215

Chapter 20: Adapting to AI's Evolution 227

Chapter 21: The Entrepreneur's Edge: AI-Powered Innovation 237

Chapter 22: AI in Health, Fitness, and Lifestyle 250

Chapter 23: Exploring New Markets with AI 262

Chapter 24: Your Creative Legacy 275

Chapter 25: Beyond the Journey: Generative AI's Role in the Future of Creativity 287

Zero to Hero: Unlocking Creativity with AI

Chapter 1: Your Hero's Journey with Generative AI

Welcome to Your Creative Adventure

Every great journey begins with a call to action. For you, that call might be a spark of curiosity about what you can create, a desire to reignite your creative spark, or the urge to turn an idea into something real. The path ahead, however, can feel overwhelming—where do you start? What tools do you need?

This is where generative AI steps in, not as a replacement for your creativity but as a collaborator. It's the trusted guide that's always ready to brainstorm, refine, and amplify your ideas. Together, you and AI can unlock possibilities you never thought possible.

Zero to Hero: Unlocking Creativity with AI

In this chapter, you'll begin to embrace the hero's journey as a framework for creativity. Whether you're here to explore new tools, solve creative challenges, or scale your skills into opportunities, your adventure starts here.

The Call to Adventure

The start of any journey is often the hardest. It's the moment you decide to leave your comfort zone and take on a new challenge. For you, the challenge might be:

- Overcoming creative doubt: "I'm not sure my ideas are good enough."

- Breaking through barriers: "I don't have the time or resources to create."

- Finding inspiration: "I don't even know where to begin."

These challenges are universal, but they don't have to hold you back. What separates heroes from bystanders is the willingness to take that first step.

Zero to Hero: Unlocking Creativity with AI

With generative AI as your ally, that step is easier than ever.

Hero Spotlight: Jane's Story

Jane was a busy parent with a passion for storytelling, but her dream of writing a children's book always felt out of reach. Between her full-time job and family commitments, the idea of starting—even brainstorming—felt impossible.

That changed when she discovered ChatGPT.

- First Steps: Jane began by asking ChatGPT for story ideas. Within minutes, she had a list of potential themes and characters.

- Building Momentum: As Jane refined her favorite idea, ChatGPT helped her develop an outline and write the first draft of her story.

- Polishing the Product: AI offered suggestions for improving dialogue, pacing, and flow, making her draft stronger with each iteration.

Zero to Hero: Unlocking Creativity with AI

Fast forward six months: Jane self-published her book on an online platform, receiving glowing reviews from parents and educators. What started as a daunting dream became a tangible reality—all because she took the first step.

Facing the Threshold of Doubt

Before you cross the threshold into action, it's normal to face doubts. What if the idea isn't good enough? What if the tools feel too complex? Heroes often encounter this inner resistance, but every step forward builds momentum.

AI Insight: Generative AI is designed to help you overcome these doubts. By breaking projects into smaller, manageable tasks, AI tools allow you to focus on progress rather than perfection.

Let's explore another example.

Hero Spotlight: Mark's First Leap

Mark was a freelance graphic designer who dreamed of expanding his services to include

Zero to Hero: Unlocking Creativity with AI

branding packages. But he worried about keeping up with client demands, especially when starting from scratch.

Generative AI became Mark's secret weapon:

- Concept Development: Mark used DALL·E to create quick logo concepts and mood boards for clients, sparking inspiration within minutes.

- Efficiency Gains: With ChatGPT, he streamlined his workflow, generating tagline ideas and mission statements for branding projects.

- Refinement: Canva allowed him to perfect designs and deliver polished, professional results.

Within three months, Mark added branding packages to his services and doubled his monthly income. AI didn't replace his creativity—it amplified it.

What to Expect from This Book

Zero to Hero: Unlocking Creativity with AI

Every journey needs a roadmap. Here's how this book will guide you from curiosity to mastery:

1. Discover the Tools: Learn about the AI platforms that will transform your creative process.

2. Take Action: Explore how to turn ideas into real-world creations with practical guidance and examples.

3. Refine and Scale: Hone your skills, grow your audience, and explore how AI can elevate your work.

4. Monetize Your Creativity: Turn your passion into profit with proven strategies and insights.

5. Future-Proof Your Process: Stay ahead of trends and evolve as technology changes.

This structure mirrors the hero's journey—starting from the call to action and culminating in mastery and legacy.

Zero to Hero: Unlocking Creativity with AI

The Hero's Journey Framework

To make your transformation feel tangible, this book is built around the timeless hero's journey. Here's how it applies to you:

1. The Call to Adventure: Recognizing your potential and embracing AI as a creative partner.

2. Discovering the Tools: Learning to use AI to brainstorm, create, and refine.

3. The Challenges: Overcoming self-doubt, technical hurdles, or creative blocks with AI's support.

4. The Hero's Transformation: Developing confidence, skill, and unique creations.

5. The Return: Sharing your success, inspiring others, and leaving a lasting legacy.

Zero to Hero: Unlocking Creativity with AI

This journey is yours to shape. Whether your goal is to write, design, innovate, or explore, you're in control of the narrative.

Interactive Challenge: Define Your Hero's Goal

Before diving into tools and techniques, let's set the foundation for your journey. Reflect on these prompts:

1. What creative goal are you hoping to achieve?

2. What's been holding you back?

3. How might AI help you overcome these challenges?

Take it further by writing your own hero's "mission statement."

- Example: "I want to create a digital portfolio that showcases my design skills, using AI to streamline the process and enhance my creativity."

Zero to Hero: Unlocking Creativity with AI

Refer back to this statement throughout your journey to stay focused on your goals.

The First Step is the Hardest

The journey from zero to hero isn't about perfection—it's about progress. With generative AI, you have the tools to turn ideas into action, overcome creative blocks, and expand your horizons.

Think of AI not as a shortcut, but as a springboard that launches your creativity further than you thought possible. In the next chapter, we'll explore the tools of the trade, showing you how to harness AI's potential and unlock your creative power.

The first step always feels the hardest, but you're not alone. You're the hero, and this is your story.

Take a moment to reflect on what you've learned in this chapter. Use these prompts to guide your thoughts:

Zero to Hero: Unlocking Creativity with AI

1. What is your personal "call to adventure"? Why do you want to explore generative AI?

2. What creative challenges or blocks have you faced in the past, and how do you hope AI can help overcome them?

3. Write down one goal you'd like to achieve by the end of this book.

Use the space below to jot down your thoughts, ideas, and reflections:

Zero to Hero: Unlocking Creativity with AI

Zero to Hero: Unlocking Creativity with AI

Chapter 2. Discovering Generative AI: The Tools of the Trade

Welcome to the Hero's Toolkit

Every hero needs the right tools to conquer their challenges. For a writer, it might be a pen; for an artist, a brush. For you, embarking on this journey into generative AI, the toolkit is revolutionary, offering endless possibilities to amplify your creativity.

This chapter introduces the most powerful tools available today, showing you how they work and how to make them work for you. Whether you're designing visuals, crafting stories, or building the next big thing, these tools are your allies, ready to bring your ideas to life.

Zero to Hero: Unlocking Creativity with AI

Why Generative AI is a Game-Changer

Generative AI isn't just another tool—it's a new way of thinking about creativity. It transforms the process by:

- Speeding up workflows: AI tools can complete tasks in minutes that used to take hours.

- Breaking through blocks: With AI, there's no such thing as running out of ideas.

- Expanding creative potential: AI can introduce concepts and designs you might not have considered.

But like any tool, it's not magic. Its power lies in how you use it. Understanding the strengths and limitations of each tool will help you wield them effectively.

The Essentials of Your Toolkit

Let's explore the tools shaping the future of creativity.

Zero to Hero: Unlocking Creativity with AI

1. Text Generation

- ChatGPT: Your partner for brainstorming, drafting, and refining text. From story ideas to ad copy, it's versatile and intuitive.

- Jasper AI: Designed for marketers, it excels at creating SEO-optimized blogs, emails, and campaigns.

2. Image Creation

- DALL·E: A pioneer in generating high-quality, imaginative visuals from text prompts. Perfect for unique designs or illustrations.

- MidJourney: Specializes in artistic and surreal images, often blending abstract and realistic styles.

3. Design Assistance

- Canva: A user-friendly platform with AI-driven templates, ideal for everything from social media posts to professional presentations.

Zero to Hero: Unlocking Creativity with AI

- RunwayML: A powerhouse for video editing, animations, and creating advanced multimedia projects.

4. Voice and Audio

- ElevenLabs: Creates realistic voiceovers for audiobooks, videos, or podcasts.

- Descript: Simplifies audio editing, transcription, and content creation for media projects.

5. Coding Support

- GitHub Copilot: Assists with writing and debugging code, helping developers work faster and more efficiently.

- Tabnine: An AI-powered code completion tool that integrates seamlessly with development workflows.

Emma's Classroom Innovation

Zero to Hero: Unlocking Creativity with AI

Emma, a high school art teacher, wanted to create engaging, visually appealing lesson plans to inspire her students. She knew she needed help but wasn't sure where to start. With generative AI, she discovered a new way to teach:

- Idea Generation: Using ChatGPT, Emma brainstormed themes for lessons, including "Exploring Surrealism" and "The Art of Modern Collage."

- Design and Visuals: She used DALL·E to generate vibrant examples of surrealist art and Canva to design polished presentations.

- Interactive Elements: Emma added AI-generated quizzes and discussion prompts, enhancing engagement.

The result? Her students were captivated, and Emma felt empowered to explore even more creative teaching methods.

How to Build Your AI Toolkit

Zero to Hero: Unlocking Creativity with AI

Not every tool is right for every creator. Here's how to build your perfect toolkit:

1. Start with a Goal:

- What are you trying to create? A short story, a design, or an entire project? Define your purpose first.

2. Experiment with Free Versions:

- Many tools offer free trials or basic plans. Start here to test their functionality without committing.

3. Pair Tools Strategically:

- Example: Use ChatGPT for brainstorming, DALL·E for visuals, and Canva for final presentation.

4. Evolve Over Time:

- As you grow, explore more advanced tools like RunwayML for video or GitHub Copilot for coding projects.

Zero to Hero: Unlocking Creativity with AI

Interactive Challenge: Create Something New

Let's put your toolkit to the test. Choose a simple project and explore how AI can enhance it:

- Step 1: Use ChatGPT to brainstorm ideas.
- Step 2: Select a visual tool (e.g., DALL·E) to generate imagery.
- Step 3: Combine everything in Canva to create a polished product.

Example Project: A social media post promoting an event.

- Brainstorm slogans with ChatGPT.
- Create event-themed visuals with DALL·E.
- Design the final post with Canva's templates.

Reflect on your experience: What surprised you? What challenges did you face?

The AI Co-Creation Framework

Think of your work with AI as a continuous cycle:

1. Inspiration: Generate raw ideas and concepts using AI prompts.

2. Iteration: Experiment and refine, shaping the output to fit your vision.

3. Creation: Blend AI-generated content with your personal touch.

4. Reflection: Assess the results, learn from the process, and prepare for the next project.

This framework ensures that AI isn't just a tool but a collaborator in your creative process.

Beyond the Basics

Zero to Hero: Unlocking Creativity with AI

Generative AI tools are constantly evolving, offering new opportunities for innovation. Consider exploring:

- RunwayML for immersive video storytelling.

- Descript for integrating audio elements into multimedia projects.

- MidJourney for abstract, gallery-worthy artwork.

The more you experiment, the more confident you'll become in weaving these tools into your creative practice.

Closing Reflection: Embrace Experimentation

Generative AI is more than just technology—it's a gateway to unlocking new dimensions of creativity. The tools introduced in this chapter are just the beginning. Start small, stay curious, and don't be afraid to experiment.

Zero to Hero: Unlocking Creativity with AI

In the next chapter, we'll dive into turning sparks of inspiration into actionable projects, guiding you from ideas to tangible results. With your toolkit in hand, you're ready to take on the world of possibilities.

After learning about the tools of the trade, take time to reflect on your creative toolkit:

1. Which AI tools mentioned in this chapter excite you the most? Why?

2. What project would you like to try first using these tools?

3. How do you think generative AI could complement your strengths as a creator?

Write your thoughts and action plan here:

Use the following page for more notes or brainstorms:

Zero to Hero: Unlocking Creativity with AI

Zero to Hero: Unlocking Creativity with AI

Zero to Hero: Unlocking Creativity with AI

Chapter 3: Turning Ideas into Action

Bridging the Gap Between Vision and Reality

Ideas are powerful. They hold the potential to inspire, create change, and leave a lasting impact. But an idea on its own is just a spark. To truly shine, it needs action.

For many creators, the hardest step isn't coming up with ideas—it's taking those first steps to bring them to life. That's where generative AI comes in. It's not just a tool for creativity; it's a catalyst for turning your vision into reality. This chapter will guide you through the process of transforming raw concepts into actionable projects, one step at a time.

From Chaos to Clarity: Organizing Your Ideas

Every great project begins with structure. It's easy to feel overwhelmed when your mind is buzzing with possibilities, but the key to moving forward is focus.

Zero to Hero: Unlocking Creativity with AI

Let's say you're working on a personal project, like designing a logo for a side hustle. Start by breaking it down:

1. Define the Goal: What's the purpose of the logo? Who is the audience?

2. Generate Options: Use ChatGPT to brainstorm styles, symbols, and taglines.

3. Select a Concept: Refine your options based on what resonates most.

Generative AI excels at organizing chaos. Tools like ChatGPT can help you outline ideas, prioritize tasks, and map out clear next steps.

Clara dreamed of hosting a music and art festival, but the sheer scale of the project paralyzed her. She wasn't sure where to begin. With AI as her creative partner, she took a series of small, intentional steps:

• Brainstorming Themes: Using ChatGPT, Clara explored possibilities like "retro

Zero to Hero: Unlocking Creativity with AI

futurism" and "eco-friendly festivals," eventually narrowing down her vision.

- Visualizing the Concept: DALL·E generated promotional visuals and stage designs, bringing her ideas to life.

- Streamlining Tasks: Clara used AI scheduling tools combined with Notion to create timelines and assign tasks.

- Promoting the Event: Canva and Jasper AI helped Clara design ads, social media posts, and email campaigns.

Within a year, her festival became a local sensation, proving that even the boldest ideas are achievable with the right mindset and tools.

The Actionable Steps Framework

When turning ideas into action, having a repeatable framework makes all the difference:

1. Start with a Prototype:

Zero to Hero: Unlocking Creativity with AI

- Use AI to create a rough draft, design, or model of your idea.

- Example: Write the opening chapter of a book or design a rough app interface.

2. Test and Refine:

- Share your prototype with a trusted audience for feedback.

- Use AI to address critiques and make improvements.

3. Commit to Milestones:

- Break your project into smaller goals, each with a timeline.

- Example: Complete a draft in two weeks, finalize designs in one month.

4. Launch and Reflect:

- Use AI tools to track success metrics and gather insights for future projects.

Zero to Hero: Unlocking Creativity with AI

Choose an idea you've been putting off and apply this framework. Create a tangible first draft within the next week.

Generative AI thrives on repetition and refinement. It allows you to iterate on ideas without getting stuck in perfectionism. For example:

- Writing: Use ChatGPT to generate multiple versions of a sentence, paragraph, or scene.

- Design: Experiment with DALL·E by tweaking prompts for fresh perspectives.

- Content Creation: Use Jasper AI to A/B test ad copy or headlines.

Iteration isn't about getting it right the first time—it's about moving closer to your vision with every attempt.

Think of yourself as a builder with your ideas serving as the blueprint. Generative AI is the set of tools you use to bring that blueprint to life. At first, the structure might seem incomplete or imperfect,

Zero to Hero: Unlocking Creativity with AI

but with each adjustment, it becomes more refined and robust.

Even the most iconic buildings started as rough sketches. Your creations will evolve, too.

Mark was a freelance designer who wanted to expand into web design but lacked experience. When his first client asked for a modern website, he leaned on AI to deliver:

1. Conceptualizing the Site: Mark used ChatGPT to generate ideas for layout, color schemes, and typography.

2. Prototyping: Canva allowed him to create wireframes, while MidJourney provided visual elements.

3. Coding Support: GitHub Copilot helped Mark write the code for interactive features, saving hours of work.

4. Client Presentation: Mark used AI tools to polish his pitch and create a stunning mockup.

Not only did the client love the site, but they also referred Mark to three new clients.

Overcoming Your First Hurdle

Take a moment to reflect on an idea you've been hesitant to start. Answer these questions:

1. What's the first step you can take to bring it to life?

2. Which AI tool could help you with that step?

3. How will you measure progress after completing it?

Commit to completing this step within the next three days.

Closing Reflection: From Idea to Action

Zero to Hero: Unlocking Creativity with AI

Taking action is often the hardest part of any journey. But with generative AI, you don't have to face that challenge alone. By breaking ideas into manageable steps, experimenting with AI tools, and iterating on your creations, you'll find momentum—and success—sooner than you think.

In the next chapter, we'll explore how to refine and scale your creations, ensuring they reach their full potential. For now, take pride in every step you've taken, no matter how small. You're on your way.

Chapter 4: Mastering the Art of Prompts

Your Call to Adventure: Becoming a Prompt Master

In every hero's journey, there comes a moment when they must learn a critical skill to succeed. For you, that skill is mastering prompts. Think of this as discovering the language that unlocks the full potential of your AI collaborator. The quality of your prompts determines whether your ideas remain vague dreams or become vividly realized creations.

This chapter is your guide to mastering this essential skill, helping you refine your communication with AI to achieve better results. From troubleshooting common issues to crafting prompts that unlock innovative possibilities, you'll gain the tools needed to advance your creative journey.

The Foundation of Prompt Crafting

Zero to Hero: Unlocking Creativity with AI

At its core, a prompt is a bridge between your vision and the AI's ability to execute it. It's the foundation of your creative process. But not all prompts are created equal. Here are the foundational principles to get you started:

1. Clarity Equals Power

- A clear prompt reduces ambiguity and ensures the AI understands your intent.

- Example: Instead of "Design a building," try "Design a futuristic skyscraper inspired by nature, with curved glass walls and eco-friendly features."

2. Provide Context

- Context helps the AI align with your vision. Include the "who," "what," and "why."

- Example: "Create a motivational speech for a graduating class of graphic designers, focusing on innovation and resilience."

Zero to Hero: Unlocking Creativity with AI

3. Set Boundaries

- Constraints direct the AI's focus and prevent irrelevant results. Specify format, tone, or length.

- Example: "Write a 300-word blog post in a professional tone, introducing a new AI-powered fitness app."

4. Encourage Creativity

- Use phrases that inspire original thinking, like "Think outside the box" or "Imagine the impossible."

- Example: "Generate a tagline for a company that designs eco-friendly spaceships. Make it bold and memorable."

Your Hero's Tool: Advanced Prompt Techniques

Zero to Hero: Unlocking Creativity with AI

Like a hero wielding a legendary weapon, you can unlock AI's true power by mastering advanced techniques.

1. Give the AI a Role

- Assigning a role helps the AI think from a specific perspective.

- Example: "You are a film director. Describe a visually stunning opening scene for a mystery thriller set in a snowy mountain town."

2. Frame Prompts as Challenges

- Encourage the AI to approach tasks as puzzles to solve.

- Example: "Write a poem in iambic pentameter that includes the themes of adventure, time travel, and self-discovery."

3. Incorporate Comparisons

- Use comparisons to guide the AI's creative direction.

- Example: "Write a pitch for a startup that combines the innovation of Tesla with the accessibility of Uber."

4. Iterate, Iterate, Iterate

- Start broad, refine your prompt based on the output, and repeat until it's perfect.

- Example: Begin with "Design a logo for a coffee shop." Refine to "Design a minimalist logo featuring a coffee cup and mountain imagery, using earthy tones."

Troubleshooting: Overcoming Prompting Pitfalls

Every hero faces challenges, and crafting prompts is no exception. Here's how to overcome common obstacles:

1. If the Output is Too Generic

- Problem: The response lacks originality.

- Solution: Add specific adjectives or constraints.

- Fix: "Generate a marketing slogan for a new smartwatch" becomes "Generate a bold, futuristic marketing slogan for a smartwatch designed for extreme sports enthusiasts."

2. If the AI Misunderstands Your Request

- Problem: The response veers off-topic.

- Solution: Reframe your prompt with more context.

- Fix: "Write a story about a cat" becomes "Write a 500-word short story about a mischievous cat who sneaks onto a spaceship and accidentally saves the day."

3. If the Output Feels Incomplete

Zero to Hero: Unlocking Creativity with AI

- Problem: The response is too short or lacks depth.

- Solution: Request specific details or expand the scope.

- Fix: "Describe a fantasy city" becomes "Describe a fantasy city in 300 words, including its architecture, culture, and transportation system."

Tying Prompts to Your Hero's Journey

Imagine your prompts as the magic spells in your hero's toolkit. Each one has the potential to unlock a different door on your journey:

- The Mentor's Guidance: Use prompts to simulate advice from experts.

- Example: "You are an art critic. Evaluate this concept for a gallery exhibit."

- The First Challenge: Craft prompts that test your ideas and refine them.

- Example: "Rewrite this paragraph as if it were narrated by a pirate."

- Crossing the Threshold: Push boundaries with daring prompts.

- Example: "Design an ad campaign for a product that doesn't exist yet. Make it feel revolutionary."

Exploring Multi-Tool Prompting

Different AI tools excel in different areas, and mastering prompts means knowing how to leverage each one:

1. ChatGPT for Storytelling

- Use structured prompts to create engaging narratives:

- Example: "Write a 5-paragraph story about a young scientist discovering a hidden world. Include a cliffhanger ending."

2. DALL·E for Visuals

- Add depth to prompts by specifying style, color, and mood:

- Example: "Create an illustration of a medieval castle at sunset, with banners flying in the wind, in the style of a fantasy oil painting."

3. Jasper AI for Marketing

- Guide the tone and focus of your copy:

- Example: "Write a persuasive Facebook ad for a plant-based energy drink targeting college students."

4. MidJourney for Art

- Think abstract to push creative limits:

- Example: "Generate a surreal artwork featuring a melting clock and a futuristic cityscape, blending elements of Salvador Dalí and cyberpunk."

Interactive Challenge: Your Prompt Crafting Masterpiece

Zero to Hero: Unlocking Creativity with AI

Select one of the following tasks and create a prompt to achieve your vision. Iterate until you're satisfied with the result:

1. Write an emotional letter from a robot to its inventor.

2. Design a futuristic fashion collection inspired by nature.

3. Generate a concept for a video game set in an underwater city.

Document your iterations and reflect on how each refinement brought you closer to your goal

Reflect on your growth as a prompt master. Use these prompts to guide your notes:

1. What's one skill or technique you've gained from this chapter?

2. How might effective prompts help you overcome creative blocks?

Zero to Hero: Unlocking Creativity with AI

3. Write down three ideas for prompts you'd like to experiment with.

Lined page here for additional notes and reflections.

Second lined page for further brainstorming.

Closing Reflection

Learning to craft effective prompts is like unlocking a secret language—one that turns ideas into reality and transforms challenges into opportunities. Master this skill, and your journey with generative AI will continue to unfold in extraordinary ways. In the next chapter, we'll explore how to refine and scale your creations, ensuring your work reaches its fullest potential.

Zero to Hero: Unlocking Creativity with AI

Zero to Hero: Unlocking Creativity with AI

Chapter 5: Overcoming Creative Blocks with AI

The Roadblock on Every Hero's Journey

Every hero encounters challenges that test their resolve. For you, as a creator, one of the most frustrating challenges is the creative block—the moments when inspiration seems to vanish, and progress feels impossible. Whether you're staring at a blank page, an unfinished design, or a stalled project, creative blocks can make even the most passionate endeavors feel daunting.

But here's the good news: with generative AI, you have a powerful ally to help you break through these roadblocks and reignite your momentum. Think of AI as the mentor or magical tool that appears just when you need it most, offering guidance, fresh perspectives, and solutions you may never have considered.

Zero to Hero: Unlocking Creativity with AI

This chapter explores practical ways to overcome creative blocks using AI, helping you transform obstacles into opportunities for growth.

Understanding Creative Blocks

Before diving into solutions, it's important to understand why creative blocks happen. They're not just about "running out of ideas." They can stem from:

1. Perfectionism: Fear of failure or not meeting high expectations.

2. Burnout: Mental exhaustion from overworking or lack of balance.

3. Overwhelm: Having too many ideas or not knowing where to start.

4. Fear of the Unknown: Uncertainty about new tools, techniques, or directions.

Zero to Hero: Unlocking Creativity with AI

Generative AI can help address each of these challenges, offering a way forward no matter what's holding you back.

Your AI Toolkit for Breaking Through Blocks

Just as every hero has a trusted weapon, you have tools at your disposal to defeat creative blocks. Here's how to wield them effectively:

1. Brainstorming with AI

- Use ChatGPT or similar tools to generate ideas when you're feeling stuck.

- Example: If you're writing a blog post, ask, "What are 10 unique angles for discussing AI in creativity?"

2. Overcoming Perfectionism

- Let AI handle the first draft.

- Example: Use Jasper AI to generate an opening paragraph or ad copy. Start with their suggestions, then refine them.

3. Simplifying Complex Problems

- Break large projects into smaller, actionable steps with AI's help.

- Example: "Create a step-by-step plan for designing a product launch campaign."

4. Visualizing Abstract Ideas

- Use DALL·E or MidJourney to turn vague concepts into tangible visuals.

- Example: "Generate an illustration of a futuristic workspace for inspiration."

5. Finding Inspiration in Unexpected Places

- Ask AI for prompts that push boundaries or blend unrelated ideas.

- Example: "What if Leonardo da Vinci designed a smartphone? Describe it."

Leo Finds His Spark

Zero to Hero: Unlocking Creativity with AI

Leo, a freelance writer, was struggling to meet a deadline. Every sentence he wrote felt forced, and he couldn't shake the feeling that his ideas were stale. Frustrated, he turned to ChatGPT for help.

- Step 1: Reframe the Problem

Leo asked ChatGPT: "What are some unconventional approaches to writing a travel article about Paris?"

- Step 2: Explore Fresh Angles

The AI suggested ideas like "A day in Paris through the eyes of a stray cat" and "The untold stories behind Parisian street art."

- Step 3: Refine the Direction

Inspired by these suggestions, Leo chose the street art angle and asked ChatGPT to outline key points for the article.

Within an hour, Leo had reignited his creativity and completed the article ahead of schedule. The

Zero to Hero: Unlocking Creativity with AI

client loved the unique perspective, and Leo gained a new technique for breaking through blocks.

Interactive Prompt: Conquer Your Block

Take a moment to think about a project where you feel stuck. Try this exercise:

1. Describe your challenge to AI as if explaining it to a mentor.

- Example: "I'm designing a logo for a coffee shop but can't decide on the style."

2. Ask for brainstorming help or specific solutions.

- Example: "Generate three logo ideas for a cozy, family-owned coffee shop."

3. Evaluate the AI's suggestions and refine your direction.

Repeat this process whenever you feel stuck, and document how AI helps you move forward.

Zero to Hero: Unlocking Creativity with AI

Building Resilience with AI

Creative blocks may never disappear entirely, but with the right strategies, you can build resilience and move through them faster:

1. Develop a Prompt Library:

    - Keep a collection of go-to prompts for brainstorming, troubleshooting, and refining ideas.

    - Example: "What's a bold headline for a campaign about sustainability?"

2. Experiment Without Judgment:

    - Use AI to test wild ideas without fear of failure. Sometimes, the best results come from unexpected places.

    - Example: "Describe a fantasy world where technology and nature coexist."

3. Celebrate Progress Over Perfection:

Zero to Hero: Unlocking Creativity with AI

- Focus on small wins. Even generating a rough idea is progress worth celebrating.

Your Hero's Growth: Transformation Through Challenges

Just as every hero emerges stronger from their trials, overcoming creative blocks with AI transforms you into a more resilient and resourceful creator. Each block is an opportunity to learn, adapt, and innovate.

Imagine yourself facing a creative block like a climber approaching a mountain. Generative AI is the gear that helps you ascend—making the climb not just possible, but empowering.

Interactive Challenge: Breaking Through Your Biggest Block

Choose a project where you're feeling stuck and ask AI to help you:

1. Identify the root cause of the block.

Zero to Hero: Unlocking Creativity with AI

2. Generate three creative solutions.

3. Create an action plan for implementing one of the solutions this week.

Reflect on how the process felt and what you learned.

Notes Section

Reflect on how you've overcome creative blocks in the past and how AI can assist moving forward. Use these prompts to guide your thoughts:

1. What's the most significant creative block you've faced recently?

2. How could generative AI help you find a new perspective or direction?

3. Write down one action step to try the next time you encounter a block.

Zero to Hero: Unlocking Creativity with AI

Closing Reflection

Creative blocks are not the end of your journey—they're a chance to grow stronger. With generative AI as your ally, you can overcome any

Zero to Hero: Unlocking Creativity with AI

obstacle and continue your transformation as a creator. In the next chapter, we'll explore how to refine and polish your creations, ensuring they reach their fullest potential.

Chapter 6: Refining and Polishing: The AI Advantage

The Hero's Forge: Where Good Becomes Great

In every hero's journey, there's a pivotal moment of transformation. For you, as a creator, this moment is the refinement process—the stage where your raw ideas are tempered, polished, and perfected. It's the difference between a good project and one that truly stands out.

Generative AI is your forge, sharpening your vision and unlocking possibilities you might not have discovered on your own. This chapter will guide you through advanced refinement techniques, practical workflows, and strategies to scale your creations, helping you achieve results you're truly proud of.

Why Refinement is the Secret to Success

Zero to Hero: Unlocking Creativity with AI

Refinement isn't just about fixing mistakes; it's about elevating your work to its highest potential. Here's why it matters:

1. Uncovering Hidden Potential: Refinement often reveals strengths or opportunities you didn't notice in the initial stages.

2. Connecting with Your Audience: Polished creations resonate more deeply and leave a lasting impression.

3. Building Confidence: A refined project reflects your best effort, boosting your pride and motivation.

But refinement can be time-consuming and, at times, overwhelming. That's where AI steps in—not to replace your vision, but to enhance it.

Advanced Refinement Techniques with AI

1. Breaking Down Refinement into Manageable Steps

Zero to Hero: Unlocking Creativity with AI

Refinement can feel daunting if you try to tackle everything at once. Use AI to break the process into smaller, actionable tasks:

- Identify Areas for Improvement: Ask ChatGPT to pinpoint weak points in a draft or design.

- Example: "What parts of this story could be more engaging?"

- Prioritize Changes: Use AI to rank the most critical edits to focus on first.

2. Iterative Feedback Loops

AI excels at providing immediate feedback. Treat it as a collaborator in your creative process:

- Refine Visuals: Use DALL·E to experiment with alternate designs, then narrow down the options.

- Test Variations: Jasper AI can generate multiple rewrites of a paragraph or tagline for comparison.

3. Enhancing Clarity and Consistency

Ensure your work flows smoothly by using AI to check for consistency:

- Writers: Test for logical flow, repetitive phrases, or gaps in your argument.

- Designers: Experiment with cohesive color schemes or balanced layouts using AI design tools.

- Entrepreneurs: Simulate customer reactions to a pitch or product description with tools like ChatGPT.

4. Adding Depth and Dimension

Refinement isn't just about fixing; it's about enriching your work:

- For Writers: Use AI to add vivid details, metaphors, or sensory descriptions.

- Example: "Rewrite this scene to make the setting feel more alive."

Zero to Hero: Unlocking Creativity with AI

- For Visual Creators: Generate variations that add textures or layers to your designs.

- For Innovators: Ask AI to suggest ways to make your idea more comprehensive or adaptable.

Maya's Transformation from Rough Draft to Masterpiece

Maya, an aspiring author, had a promising but underwhelming short story. She felt her descriptions lacked depth and the pacing dragged in key moments. Using generative AI, Maya transformed her draft:

1. Identifying Problem Areas: She asked ChatGPT to summarize each paragraph, helping her pinpoint where the narrative lost momentum.

2. Enriching Descriptions: Using AI-generated suggestions, Maya added sensory details to her settings and characters.

3. Testing Pacing: Maya used ChatGPT to suggest reordering certain scenes for better flow.

4. Iterating with Feedback: After incorporating the changes, she asked the AI for a final review, receiving suggestions to fine-tune dialogue.

The result? A short story that captivated her critique group and landed her first submission acceptance.

Scaling Refinement: Working Smarter, Not Harder

Refinement doesn't have to stop with a single project. Generative AI allows you to scale your efforts, ensuring your work remains sharp across multiple platforms or iterations.

1. Automate Repetitive Tasks

AI tools can streamline repetitive elements of the refinement process, freeing your time for creativity:

- **Proofreading and Grammar Checks:** Use Grammarly or ChatGPT to clean up your writing.

- **Design Adjustments:** Automate resizing or reformatting visuals for different platforms.

2. Create Consistent Variations

Scaling often means adapting your work for new audiences or formats. AI makes this easy:

- **For Writers:** Turn a blog post into a LinkedIn article or Twitter thread.

- **For Designers:** Use Canva's AI tools to generate design variations tailored to specific platforms.

- **For Entrepreneurs:** Adapt your pitch for different audiences, such as investors or customers.

3. Leverage Data for Refinement

Zero to Hero: Unlocking Creativity with AI

AI-powered analytics tools can provide valuable insights to guide your refinement process:

- Use Jasper AI to analyze which headlines or captions resonate most with audiences.

- Track engagement metrics to identify areas for improvement.

The Future of Refinement with AI

The refinement process is poised to become even more intuitive as AI evolves:

1. Real-Time Collaboration: Imagine tools that offer instant suggestions as you work.

2. Style Personalization: AI will learn your preferences, offering recommendations tailored to your unique voice or design style.

3. Dynamic Feedback: Future AI systems may simulate audience reactions in real-time, helping you predict impact before release.

Interactive Challenge: From Rough to Radiant

Zero to Hero: Unlocking Creativity with AI

Choose a current project and follow these steps to refine it:

1. Ask for AI Feedback: Identify three areas for improvement.

2. Experiment with Changes: Use AI to test multiple refinements for one of these areas.

3. Evaluate and Iterate: Compare your original version with the refined result. Which changes made the biggest impact?

Notes Section

Reflect on your creative process and how refinement plays a role. Use these prompts to guide your thoughts:

1. What's one project that could benefit from immediate refinement?

2. Which AI tools or techniques are you most excited to try for polishing your work?

3. Write down three specific refinement goals you'd like to achieve this month.

Zero to Hero: Unlocking Creativity with AI

Closing Reflection

Refinement is where the magic happens. It's where your creative potential shines brightest and where your unique voice comes to life. With

Zero to Hero: Unlocking Creativity with AI generative AI as your partner, you're equipped to tackle any challenge and elevate your work to its fullest potential. In the next chapter, we'll explore how to scale your creative efforts, ensuring your work reaches and resonates with a larger audience.

Chapter 7: Scaling Your Efforts: Beyond the First Creation

The Hero's Next Challenge: Scaling to New Heights

In the hero's journey, achieving the first victory is only the beginning. The next step is expanding that success—scaling efforts to reach greater heights and have a lasting impact. For creators, scaling means moving beyond one-off successes to build systems, communities, and projects that grow sustainably over time.

Scaling isn't just about growing bigger—it's about growing smarter. It's about reaching more people, unlocking new opportunities, and making your work resonate on a broader scale. With generative AI, you have a powerful ally to help you do this efficiently and creatively.

Why Scaling Matters in the Creative Journey

Scaling transforms your work from a personal achievement into a platform for impact. Here's why it's a critical part of your journey:

1. Broadening Your Reach: Scaling allows your work to touch more lives and make a bigger difference.

2. Diversifying Opportunities: As your efforts grow, so do your chances to explore new formats, platforms, and collaborations.

3. Building Sustainability: By creating scalable systems, you ensure your creative journey can continue without burning out or losing momentum.

Generative AI simplifies the scaling process, allowing you to focus on what matters most: your vision and creativity.

Scaling Strategies for Long-Term Growth

1. Expanding Formats

Repurposing your work for different formats is one of the simplest ways to scale:

- Example for Writers: Turn a blog post into an e-book, audiobook, or video script. Use tools like Jasper AI to adapt the content for each medium.

- Example for Designers: Transform a visual design into merchandise, templates, or digital assets for sale.

- Example for Entrepreneurs: Convert a product demo into a webinar series or online course.

2. Building an Ecosystem

Instead of focusing on individual projects, create an interconnected ecosystem:

- Content Creators: Build a portfolio where each piece links to others, such as articles that promote a book or video series.

• Product Designers: Develop complementary products or services to enhance the value of your main offering.

• Service Providers: Create packages that combine services, adding scalability without additional workload.

3. Leveraging AI for Personalization

Personalization helps your audience feel directly connected to your work:

• Use AI to create tailored recommendations or experiences for different audience segments.

• Example: A writer could use AI to generate personalized newsletters based on reader preferences.

• Localize your content for international audiences with AI translation tools like DeepL.

Zero to Hero: Unlocking Creativity with AI

Advanced Scaling Techniques with AI

1. Automating Repetitive Tasks

Scaling often requires handling repetitive tasks that eat into creative time. AI can automate:

- Social Media Posting: Use platforms like Buffer to schedule and optimize posts.

- Customer Communication: Implement chatbots for FAQs or initial inquiries.

- Content Customization: Automatically adjust visuals, formats, or tone to suit different platforms.

2. Exploring Collaboration Opportunities

Scaling doesn't mean doing it all alone. Use AI to identify and facilitate collaborations:

- Find potential partners or collaborators by analyzing shared interests or audience overlaps.

Zero to Hero: Unlocking Creativity with AI

- Generate pitches tailored to each collaborator, emphasizing mutual benefits.

3. Scaling Through Community Building

A strong community is one of the most effective ways to scale sustainably. AI tools can help you:

- Engage audiences with personalized responses or content recommendations.

- Host virtual events or forums, using AI moderation to keep discussions constructive.

- Create gamified elements, such as rewards for participation, to encourage loyalty.

James Builds a Creative Empire

James, a self-taught musician, began his journey by producing lo-fi beats in his bedroom. His first track gained modest traction on a streaming platform, but James wanted to do more than release singles—he wanted to build a brand.

Zero to Hero: Unlocking Creativity with AI

1. Repurposing Content: James used AI tools to turn his tracks into relaxing background videos for YouTube and social media loops for TikTok.

2. Building a Community: He created a Discord server where fans could share playlists and ideas, using AI to suggest engaging topics and moderate discussions.

3. Expanding Formats: James collaborated with AI-powered design tools to create album art, merchandise, and digital collectibles.

4. Automating Outreach: Using AI analytics, James targeted his most engaged listeners with personalized messages about upcoming releases.

Within two years, James had grown his music into a multi-platform brand, generating income from streaming, merchandise, and live events.

Scaling Pitfalls to Avoid

Zero to Hero: Unlocking Creativity with AI

Scaling comes with its own set of challenges. Here's how to navigate them:

1. Overextension: Trying to do too much at once can lead to burnout.

- Solution: Focus on one scalable system or platform at a time.

2. Losing Authenticity: Scaling too quickly can dilute your unique voice or vision.

- Solution: Use AI to maintain consistency in tone and style across formats.

3. Neglecting Quality: Expanding reach should never come at the cost of quality.

- Solution: Use AI to refine and polish your work at each stage of scaling.

The Future of Creative Scaling with AI

The future of scaling will be driven by innovations in AI, offering creators even more opportunities to grow:

Zero to Hero: Unlocking Creativity with AI

1. Adaptive Scaling Models: AI will allow creators to scale dynamically, adjusting strategies in real time based on audience feedback.

2. AI-Driven Market Insights: Advanced analytics will help identify emerging trends, niches, and opportunities for expansion.

3. Seamless Multimodal Integration: The ability to combine text, visuals, and audio in a single workflow will unlock unprecedented scalability.

Interactive Challenge: Scaling Your Vision

Think of a project or creation you've completed, and brainstorm ways to scale it:

1. Identify at least three new formats or platforms for your work.

2. Use AI to automate one aspect of the scaling process, such as creating templates or analyzing audience data.

3. Set a measurable goal, such as doubling your audience reach or generating a specific income milestone.

Reflect on how scaling changes your perspective on your work and its potential.

Notes Section

Use these prompts to brainstorm and reflect on your scaling strategies:

1. What's one project you've completed that has the potential to scale?

2. How could AI tools help you expand your reach or automate your efforts?

3. Write down three action steps to start scaling your work today.

Zero to Hero: Unlocking Creativity with AI

Closing Reflection

Scaling is where your creativity meets its broader purpose, expanding your impact and creating lasting value. With AI as your partner, the

Zero to Hero: Unlocking Creativity with AI
possibilities for growth are endless. In the next chapter, we'll explore the ethics of AI in creativity, ensuring your journey is both innovative and responsible.

Chapter 8: The Ethics of AI in Creativity

The Hero's Compass: Navigating the Ethics of AI

Every hero faces decisions that test their character. As you embrace generative AI, ethical questions become part of your journey. How do you ensure your use of AI respects others' rights? How do you navigate its societal impacts and maintain trust with your audience?

In this chapter, we'll explore ethical challenges, provide actionable strategies, and encourage you to forge your own moral code as a creator. Think of this as your compass—a guide to making decisions that not only elevate your work but also contribute positively to the creative world.

Why Ethics Are Essential to the Creative Journey

Ethics are the foundation of responsible AI use. They're not just about avoiding harm; they're about enhancing the value of your work and its impact. Here's why they matter:

1. Upholding Integrity: Ethical practices protect your reputation and foster trust with your audience.

2. Fostering Innovation: By respecting intellectual property and diversity, you encourage creativity and originality in your field.

3. Empowering Collaboration: Ethical AI use builds bridges between creators, audiences, and the tools we rely on.

4. Contributing to Society: Responsible AI use ensures technology benefits everyone, not just a privileged few.

The Four Pillars of Ethical AI Creativity

These pillars serve as your foundation for navigating the ethical challenges of generative AI:

Zero to Hero: Unlocking Creativity with AI

1. Intellectual Property and Fair Use

AI tools draw from vast datasets, often including copyrighted works. Misuse of these can lead to legal and ethical concerns.

- The Challenge: Ensuring originality and respecting others' work.

- Best Practices:

- Choose AI tools that disclose their training data.

- Avoid using AI to directly mimic or replicate another creator's style.

- Credit AI as a collaborator where appropriate.

- Example: Instead of "This is my original creation," say, "This image was created with MidJourney and enhanced by me."

2. Fairness and Inclusivity

Zero to Hero: Unlocking Creativity with AI

AI systems often reflect biases present in their training data. It's your responsibility to ensure your work promotes fairness.

- The Challenge: Avoiding stereotypes and ensuring representation.

- Best Practices:

- Test AI outputs for unintended bias.

- Write prompts that emphasize diversity and inclusivity.

- Example: When creating character designs, specify, "Include a range of ages, ethnicities, and abilities."

3. Transparency and Accountability

Audiences value honesty about how your work is created. Transparency builds trust and educates others.

- The Challenge: Balancing disclosure with creativity.

Zero to Hero: Unlocking Creativity with AI

- Best Practices:

    - Clearly communicate how AI contributed to your work.

    - Share your process to demystify AI for your audience.

    - Example: "This story's draft was generated by ChatGPT and refined by me for tone and pacing."

4. Responsible Automation

Automation should enhance human creativity, not replace it. Using AI responsibly ensures you maintain the personal touch in your work.

- The Challenge: Avoiding over-reliance on AI.

- Best Practices:

    - Use AI for repetitive or technical tasks, freeing yourself to focus on creativity.

Zero to Hero: Unlocking Creativity with AI

- Pair AI-generated ideas with human refinement for a unique blend of innovation.

- Example: "I used AI to brainstorm ideas, but the final execution is entirely my own."

Practical Strategies for Staying Ethical

1. Set Clear Guidelines

Create a personal code of ethics for your AI use. For example:

- Credit AI contributions.

- Avoid imitating specific creators without permission.

- Test outputs for potential bias.

2. Collaborate Thoughtfully

AI works best as a partner, not a replacement. Use it to:

- Save time on repetitive tasks.

Zero to Hero: Unlocking Creativity with AI

- Expand your creative options.

- Generate ideas you might not have considered on your own.

3. Educate Your Audience

Transparency can be a powerful tool. Share your creative process, including how AI contributed. This builds trust and helps others understand AI's potential.

4. Stay Informed

AI technology evolves rapidly. Keep up with developments in:

- Ethical standards.

- New tools and their capabilities.

- Discussions about AI's impact on creativity and society.

Noah's Ethical Breakthrough

Zero to Hero: Unlocking Creativity with AI

Noah, a graphic designer, was approached by a client who wanted a logo "in the style of a famous artist." Noah faced a dilemma: the client's request risked infringing on the original artist's intellectual property.

- Step 1: Reframing the Request

Noah explained the importance of originality and proposed a design inspired by the artist's techniques rather than a direct imitation.

- Step 2: Leveraging AI Responsibly

Using generative AI, Noah created abstract visuals based on the client's concept and combined them with his own sketches to produce a unique logo.

- Step 3: Educating the Client

Noah shared his process, highlighting the ethical considerations involved.

The client appreciated Noah's transparency and professionalism, and the final logo became a standout piece in Noah's portfolio.

Emerging Ethical Challenges

As AI advances, new ethical questions arise:

1. Deepfakes and Misinformation

- AI can create convincing but false media.

- Tip: Use your skills to promote truth and avoid contributing to misinformation.

2. Ownership of AI-Created Works

- Who owns AI-generated content—the user or the tool's creator?

- Tip: Read terms of service carefully and maintain documentation of your process.

3. Accessibility and Equity

Zero to Hero: Unlocking Creativity with AI

- AI tools may not be accessible to everyone due to cost or technical barriers.

- Tip: Advocate for affordable and inclusive AI solutions.

Interactive Challenge: Craft Your AI Compass

Reflect on your values and how they apply to AI use. Write your own AI ethics guidelines:

1. How will you ensure fairness and inclusivity in your creations?

2. What steps will you take to remain transparent about AI's role in your process?

3. How can you balance automation with personal creativity?

Post your guidelines somewhere visible as a reminder to stay true to your values.

Notes Section

Zero to Hero: Unlocking Creativity with AI

Use these prompts to reflect on your approach to AI ethics:

1. What's one ethical dilemma you've faced while using AI?

2. How can ethical practices enhance your creativity and audience trust?

3. Write down three actions you'll take to promote ethical AI use in your field.

Closing Reflection

Ethics are the cornerstone of your creative journey. By using AI responsibly, you ensure that your work not only reaches its highest potential but

Zero to Hero: Unlocking Creativity with AI

also contributes positively to the creative landscape. In the next chapter, we'll explore how to build your personal and professional brand with AI, helping you share your vision with the world.

Chapter 9: Building Personal and Professional Branding with AI

The Hero's Identity: Crafting a Brand That Resonates

Every hero in a story has an identity—a unique symbol or reputation that makes them unforgettable. For creators, your brand is that identity. It's the combination of what you do, how you do it, and why people connect with your work.

Generative AI is the ultimate ally for building and elevating your personal or professional brand. It can amplify your message, streamline your process, and help you engage with audiences in ways that feel authentic and impactful. In this chapter, we'll explore how to leverage AI tools to create a brand that not only stands out but also grows with you on your creative journey.

Why Branding is Crucial for Creators

Your brand is more than a logo or tagline—it's the emotional connection you create with your audience. A strong brand:

1. Differentiates You: Your brand sets you apart in a crowded market.

2. Builds Trust: Consistency and authenticity foster loyalty and credibility.

3. Drives Engagement: A well-defined brand inspires people to follow, share, and support your work.

Branding isn't just for entrepreneurs or businesses; it's for anyone who wants their creative efforts to leave a lasting impact. With AI, branding becomes more accessible, creative, and effective.

The Foundations of a Strong Brand

To build a brand that resonates, you need a clear foundation:

1. Know Your 'Why'

Zero to Hero: Unlocking Creativity with AI

Your purpose is the heart of your brand. AI can help you articulate it:

- Prompt Example: "Help me write a mission statement for a brand focused on empowering small businesses with affordable design solutions."

- Refine your responses until your mission feels authentic and personal.

2. Define Your Audience

Understanding your audience is key to crafting a brand that connects. Use AI tools to:

- Analyze audience data and demographics.

- Segment your audience into groups with tailored messages.

- Example: "What are common interests among eco-conscious consumers aged 25–35?"

3. Identify Your Unique Value

What makes you different? AI can help uncover or articulate your unique strengths:

- Use AI-powered surveys or social listening tools to gather feedback.

- Experiment with positioning statements, such as "I create [X] for [Y] in a way that [Z]."

Building a Cohesive Visual Brand with AI

1. Designing a Logo That Speaks for You

A logo is often the first thing people associate with your brand. Use AI tools like Looka or Canva to:

- Generate initial concepts based on your preferences.

- Refine colors, typography, and layout to align with your values.

Zero to Hero: Unlocking Creativity with AI

2. Creating a Signature Style

AI can help you establish a consistent look across all platforms:

- **Color Palettes:** Use tools like Coolors or Adobe Color to find color schemes that evoke the right emotions.

- **Templates:** Create reusable templates for social media, emails, and presentations.

- **Visual Elements:** Experiment with AI-generated art to add a unique flair to your branding.

3. Adapting for Multiple Formats

Your visuals need to look great everywhere—websites, social media, print, and more. AI can automate resizing and optimization, ensuring your brand remains consistent.

Crafting an Engaging Voice with AI

1. Finding Your Brand Voice

Your tone and style should reflect your personality and values. AI can help you:

- Experiment with different tones, from professional to playful.

- Analyze competitors' messaging to find gaps or opportunities.

2. Maintaining Consistency Across Channels

Consistency is key to building trust. Use AI tools like Jasper to ensure your tone stays uniform across platforms.

- Example Prompt: "Rewrite this post to match a tone that's friendly and approachable."

3. Creating Evergreen Content

Evergreen content builds long-term value for your brand. Use AI to:

- Generate blog posts, tutorials, or guides that remain relevant over time.

- Repurpose this content into infographics, videos, or social media posts.

Advanced Branding Strategies with AI

1. Hyper-Personalization

AI enables you to tailor messages for individual audience segments:

- Example: Use AI to send personalized email campaigns based on user behavior.
- Leverage recommendation engines to suggest products or content aligned with user preferences.

2. Building an Interactive Brand Experience

Interactive content drives engagement and creates memorable experiences:

- Use AI to create quizzes, polls, or challenges that reflect your brand.

- Example: "What type of [X] are you?" quiz for your audience.

3. Monitoring and Evolving Your Brand

AI analytics tools help you track how your brand is performing:

- Monitor mentions, shares, and feedback in real-time.
- Use insights to adapt your branding strategy and stay ahead of trends.

Raj's Professional Rebrand

Raj, an architect, wanted to transition from traditional projects to sustainable design consulting. However, his existing brand didn't reflect his new direction. Here's how AI helped him reinvent himself:

1. Defining His Vision: Raj used ChatGPT to brainstorm brand values, emphasizing sustainability and innovation.

2. Designing a New Visual Identity: With Canva's AI tools, he created a sleek logo featuring eco-friendly symbols and a modern color palette.

3. Building Thought Leadership: Raj used Jasper AI to write LinkedIn articles on green architecture, positioning himself as an expert.

4. Personalizing Outreach: AI-powered email campaigns targeted developers and urban planners interested in sustainable solutions.

Within a year, Raj's new brand attracted high-profile clients, allowing him to fully transition into his desired niche.

Future Trends in AI Branding

The branding landscape is evolving rapidly, with AI at the forefront. Here's what's coming:

1. AI-Generated Influencers: Virtual influencers with unique personalities will become part of brand campaigns.

2. Dynamic Branding: Real-time AI will adapt your brand's visuals or messaging based on current trends.

3. Global Personalization: AI translation and localization will make it easier to build a global brand.

Interactive Challenge: Build Your AI-Powered Brand

Take these steps to start building or refining your brand with AI:

1. Clarify Your Identity: Use AI to brainstorm your mission, values, and audience profile.

2. Create Visual Assets: Design a logo, templates, or visuals that reflect your brand.

3. Plan Your Content: Use AI to draft a content calendar with posts, articles, and campaigns tailored to your audience.

Zero to Hero: Unlocking Creativity with AI

Reflect on how these steps enhance your brand and set goals for the next stage of your journey.

Notes Section

Reflect on your branding goals and strategies. Use these prompts to guide your thoughts:

1. What's the story behind your brand?

2. How could AI tools make your branding efforts more effective?

3. Write down three specific actions you'll take to refine or expand your brand.

Zero to Hero: Unlocking Creativity with AI

Closing Reflection

Your brand is your creative identity, the way you connect with the world. With generative AI, you can craft a brand that's authentic, impactful, and ready to grow with you. In the next chapter, we'll explore how to turn your creative passion into a sustainable business, helping you take the next step in your hero's journey.

Chapter 10: From Passion to Profession: Launching Your AI-Powered Business

The Hero's Leap: Turning Dreams into Reality

In every hero's journey, there comes a pivotal moment—a leap of faith that transforms potential into action. For you, that moment is turning your passion into a profession. It's about shifting from creating for enjoyment to building a sustainable business that reflects your unique vision and delivers value to the world.

Generative AI is not just a tool for creation; it's a partner in innovation. It can help you launch, grow, and scale your business by automating tasks, personalizing outreach, and unlocking opportunities you never thought possible. This chapter is your roadmap to building an AI-powered business from the ground up, empowering you to share your creativity while ensuring long-term success.

Zero to Hero: Unlocking Creativity with AI

Why Now is the Time for AI-Powered Businesses

The intersection of creativity and technology is reshaping industries and lowering barriers to entrepreneurship. Here's why embracing AI in your business is a game-changer:

1. Access to Advanced Tools: AI-powered platforms like Jasper, Canva, and ChatGPT make professional-grade resources available to anyone.

2. Efficiency at Scale: By automating repetitive tasks, AI allows you to focus on strategy and innovation.

3. Hyper-Personalization: Tailor your products and messages to individual customer needs, creating a more engaging and memorable experience.

4. Global Reach: AI translation and localization tools enable you to expand beyond borders without additional overhead.

The opportunity is ripe to build a business that reflects your creative passion while leveraging the efficiency and adaptability of AI.

The Roadmap to Launching Your AI-Powered Business

Step 1: Define Your Business Vision

Every successful business begins with a clear vision. Your vision is the "why" behind your work, guiding your decisions and keeping you aligned with your goals.

- Clarify Your Purpose:

Use AI tools to brainstorm ideas for what your business will offer.

- Prompt Example: "Help me define a mission for a business that uses AI to create educational resources for kids."

- Identify Your Niche:

AI analytics can help you spot underserved markets or trends in your industry.

- Example: If you're a photographer, AI might reveal a growing demand for drone-based real estate imagery.

- Articulate Your Goals:

Write down both short-term and long-term goals for your business. AI tools like Notion or Trello can help organize and track your progress.

Step 2: Validate Your Idea

Before committing resources, ensure there's demand for your product or service. Validation reduces risk and sets you up for success.

- Market Research with AI:

Zero to Hero: Unlocking Creativity with AI

Tools like Google Trends and Semrush use AI to analyze industry trends and keywords.

- Example: "What's the search volume for AI-powered logo design services?"

- Conduct AI-Powered Surveys:

Platforms like Typeform can create engaging surveys to gather feedback from potential customers.

- Ask questions like, "What features would you value most in a subscription service for writing prompts?"

- Competitor Analysis:

Use tools like SimilarWeb to analyze competitors' strategies, pricing models, and customer reviews. Identify gaps you can fill.

Step 3: Build a Scalable Workflow

Your workflow is the backbone of your business. AI can optimize every step, allowing you to scale efficiently.

Zero to Hero: Unlocking Creativity with AI

- Content Creation Automation:

Tools like Jasper AI and Hootsuite can streamline content creation and scheduling.

- Example: "Schedule 30 days of social media posts promoting my new e-book launch."

- Customer Relationship Management (CRM):

Platforms like HubSpot use AI to track customer interactions and suggest personalized follow-ups.

- Example: "Send a thank-you email three days after purchase with a 10% discount code for their next order."

- Inventory and Financial Management:

Use AI tools like QuickBooks to manage expenses, generate invoices, and forecast revenue.

Step 4: Create a Digital Presence

Zero to Hero: Unlocking Creativity with AI

Your online presence is your storefront, and first impressions matter. Use AI to create a professional, cohesive, and engaging digital identity.

- Website Creation:

Platforms like Wix and Squarespace use AI to guide you through building a website that's visually appealing and user-friendly.

- SEO Optimization:

Tools like Surfer SEO and Ahrefs can analyze your website's performance and recommend improvements to boost visibility.

- Email Marketing:

Use AI to craft personalized email campaigns that resonate with your audience.

- Example Prompt: "Create an email sequence welcoming new subscribers to my blog about sustainable living."

Step 5: Launch and Iterate

Zero to Hero: Unlocking Creativity with AI

Launching your business is just the beginning. The key to growth is learning from feedback and adapting your strategies.

- Minimum Viable Product (MVP):

Start with a simplified version of your offering to test the market.

- Example: Launch a small product line or a limited service package.

- AI Analytics for Feedback:

Use tools like Google Analytics to track performance and identify areas for improvement.

- Monitor metrics like website traffic, conversion rates, and customer retention.

- Continuous Improvement:

Regularly refine your offerings based on customer input and market trends.

Mia's Creative Business Journey

Zero to Hero: Unlocking Creativity with AI

Mia, a former teacher, turned her love for writing into an AI-powered business. She wanted to create educational resources for teachers and parents but didn't know where to start.

1. Defining Her Vision:

Mia used ChatGPT to brainstorm a mission statement: "Empowering educators with engaging, AI-enhanced learning tools."

2. Validating Her Idea:

She conducted surveys to identify the most in-demand resources, such as interactive lesson plans and creative writing prompts.

3. Building Her Workflow:

Mia used Jasper AI to generate draft lesson plans, which she customized for different grade levels.

4. Creating Her Digital Presence:

Zero to Hero: Unlocking Creativity with AI

Canva helped Mia design a polished website and social media templates.

5. Launching and Iterating:

After launching her product line, Mia used customer feedback to refine her offerings and expand into digital workshops.

Within 18 months, Mia's side project became a full-time business, earning her accolades in the education community.

Interactive Challenge: Create Your Business Blueprint

Ready to turn your passion into a profession? Use this step-by-step guide:

1. Define Your Mission: Write a mission statement that reflects your goals and values.

2. Identify AI Tools: List three AI tools that will streamline your workflow.

3. Plan Your Launch: Set a timeline with actionable steps to bring your business to life.

Notes Section

Reflect on your entrepreneurial goals. Use these prompts to guide your thoughts:

1. What's one idea you're passionate about turning into a business?

2. How could AI tools simplify or enhance your workflow?

3. Write down three milestones to measure your success.

Lined page here for additional notes and reflections.

Second lined page for brainstorming or planning.

Zero to Hero: Unlocking Creativity with AI

Closing Reflection

Launching an AI-powered business is a leap of courage, creativity, and strategy. With the tools and insights in this chapter, you're ready to take your passion to the next level and make your vision a reality. In the next chapter, we'll explore how generative AI is transforming education, opening up new opportunities for learning and innovation.

Zero to Hero: Unlocking Creativity with AI

Chapter 11: Generative AI in Education and Learning

The Hero as a Lifelong Learner

Every great hero is also a learner, gaining wisdom from challenges and growth through knowledge. Whether you're a student, teacher, or someone simply curious about the world, learning is a constant. But the way we learn is evolving.

Generative AI has introduced tools that adapt to individual needs, foster creativity, and make learning more interactive than ever. From personalized study paths to time-saving tools for educators, AI has the potential to transform education into an experience as dynamic as the learner themselves.

This chapter is your guide to understanding how AI is reshaping education and how you can use it to build skills, teach effectively, and stay curious throughout your journey.

Zero to Hero: Unlocking Creativity with AI

How AI Elevates Learning

AI's role in education goes beyond efficiency—it's about empowerment:

1. Tailored Learning Paths: AI identifies and adapts to individual strengths and weaknesses, making education truly personalized.

2. Expanded Accessibility: By breaking down barriers like language, cost, or disability, AI ensures education reaches more people.

3. Engagement Through Interactivity: Tools powered by AI make lessons more fun, interactive, and hands-on.

4. Scaling Creativity: Educators can focus more on innovation and mentorship while AI handles repetitive tasks.

AI as a Personalized Learning Partner

1. Adaptive Study Plans

Zero to Hero: Unlocking Creativity with AI

AI platforms create dynamic learning experiences that grow with the user:

- Example: A language-learning app adjusts its difficulty based on how well you perform, ensuring progress without overwhelming you.

- Tools: Duolingo (languages), Khan Academy (varied subjects), and Cerego (memory mastery).

- How It Works: These tools analyze your strengths and weaknesses through data, then suggest a path forward.

- Real-World Impact: A student struggling with algebra can focus on foundational concepts before moving on to complex problems.

2. Real-Time Feedback for Mastery

One of AI's most valuable contributions is its ability to provide immediate feedback:

Zero to Hero: Unlocking Creativity with AI

- Grammarly doesn't just fix typos—it explains the rules behind the corrections, helping students write better over time.

- Socrative allows teachers to create quizzes that provide instant results and insights into class-wide comprehension levels.

3. Exploration Beyond the Classroom

Curiosity drives learning, and AI opens doors to countless resources:

- Ask ChatGPT to break down Shakespeare's Hamlet or help you write a poem in the same style.

- Use AI tools like WolframAlpha to answer complex math problems with step-by-step explanations.

AI as a Transformational Tool for Educators

1. Automating the Routine

Zero to Hero: Unlocking Creativity with AI

Educators often spend hours grading or preparing materials—AI can lighten this load:

- Gradescope automates the grading process for essays, assignments, and exams while maintaining fairness and consistency.

- Canva's AI tools generate polished visual aids, lesson plans, and slides within minutes.

2. Crafting Inclusive and Engaging Content

AI enhances accessibility and engagement:

- Example: Create interactive lessons with tools like Kahoot! or Nearpod, which use AI to adapt quizzes and activities to class needs.

- Text-to-speech apps like NaturalReader help students with visual impairments engage with course material.

3. Mentorship Over Memorization

AI frees up time for educators to focus on what matters most—mentorship. By handling repetitive

Zero to Hero: Unlocking Creativity with AI

tasks, teachers can spend more energy on fostering creativity and critical thinking.

Emily's Story: Transforming the Classroom with AI

Emily, a high school biology teacher, knew her students were struggling with the traditional teaching format. Concepts like genetics and ecosystems felt abstract and overwhelming. Determined to make learning exciting and relatable, Emily turned to generative AI.

- Step 1: Creating Visuals That Captivate

Emily used DALL·E to generate unique, vibrant visuals of DNA structures and food webs. These images brought abstract concepts to life.

- Step 2: Personalizing Assignments

ChatGPT allowed Emily to create tiered assignments. Advanced students explored genetic editing, while others focused on foundational genetics, ensuring all students were challenged at their level.

- Step 3: Simulating Real-World Scenarios

With AI-powered VR tools, Emily introduced simulations where students "explored" rainforest ecosystems, observing food chain interactions firsthand.

- Step 4: Engaging Feedback Loops

AI-based quizzes provided Emily with instant insights, allowing her to adjust her teaching in real-time.

- Results: Attendance improved, students reported increased confidence in biology, and Emily herself rediscovered her passion for teaching.

Advanced AI Applications in Education

1. Immersive Learning with VR and AR

Combining AI with augmented and virtual reality brings lessons to life:

• Explore a 3D model of the human body, guided by an AI assistant explaining each organ's function.

• Travel back in time to ancient civilizations, interacting with AI-generated characters who share historical context.

2. AI-Driven Peer Collaboration

AI connects students globally, fostering collaborative problem-solving:

• Example: Two students from different countries work on a joint science project, guided by AI tools that translate languages and suggest solutions.

3. Data-Driven Curriculum Development

AI analyzes classroom performance to suggest changes in teaching strategies:

- Example: A teacher notices that most students struggle with fractions and uses AI to redesign the lesson with new examples and interactive exercises.

The Future of AI in Education

1. Lifelong Learning Ecosystems: AI will offer personalized learning paths that span decades, evolving with individuals' goals and careers.

2. Hyper-Personalized Content: AI will adapt entire curriculums to suit learning preferences, from auditory learners to hands-on practitioners.

3. Ethical Challenges: As AI plays a bigger role, ethical considerations—like data privacy and algorithmic bias—must be addressed.

Interactive Challenge: Designing Your AI Learning Plan

Try these steps to enhance your learning with AI:

Zero to Hero: Unlocking Creativity with AI

1. Choose a skill or topic you've always wanted to learn.

2. Use an AI tool to create a personalized roadmap for mastering that topic.

3. Experiment with AI-powered resources, such as quizzes, simulations, or writing aids.

Write about your experience and reflect on how AI made learning more engaging or efficient.

Notes Section

Reflect on your educational journey with AI. Use these prompts to guide your thoughts:

1. What's one learning challenge you've faced, and how could AI help address it?

2. What tools or methods can you use to make learning more accessible to others?

3. Write down three topics you'd like to explore using AI.

Zero to Hero: Unlocking Creativity with AI

Zero to Hero: Unlocking Creativity with AI

Closing Reflection

Education is more than memorizing facts—it's about curiosity, growth, and connection. Generative AI is reshaping how we learn and teach, offering tools to make education dynamic and accessible for all. As you continue your journey, think of how you can use these tools to not only learn but also empower others. In the next chapter, we'll explore the future of storytelling with AI, where creativity and technology collide to create unforgettable narratives.

Zero to Hero: Unlocking Creativity with AI

Chapter 12: The Future of Storytelling with AI

The Hero's Power to Shape Narratives

Every culture, every movement, and every individual has been shaped by stories. They're how we connect, remember, and dream. But now, storytelling itself is undergoing a transformation. With the advent of generative AI, creators are equipped to not only tell stories but to build worlds, interact with audiences in real-time, and craft narratives that evolve and adapt.

Generative AI empowers creators to break free from traditional formats, exploring new ways to engage and inspire. From adaptive narratives to fully immersive worlds, AI transforms how we consume, create, and connect through stories. This chapter takes a deeper dive into these revolutionary shifts and how you can harness them.

Zero to Hero: Unlocking Creativity with AI

AI in Storytelling: A Tool, Not a Replacement

A common fear is that AI might replace human creativity. In truth, it amplifies it. Just as a paintbrush doesn't define an artist, AI doesn't replace the storyteller—it enhances their vision. Here's how:

1. AI as a Collaborator: Think of AI as a brainstorming partner, generating ideas and refining your concepts.

2. AI as a Craftsman: It handles time-consuming tasks, like editing or formatting, so you can focus on creativity.

3. AI as an Innovator: It introduces possibilities that may not have crossed your mind, from branching narratives to procedurally generated worlds.

AI-Driven Storytelling Across Mediums

1. Literature: From Novels to Dynamic E-Books

Zero to Hero: Unlocking Creativity with AI

AI tools are revolutionizing how we write and consume literature:

• Dynamic E-Books: Imagine a novel that changes based on your mood or preferences. For example, an AI-generated fantasy novel could offer different endings depending on whether the reader prefers a tragic or triumphant resolution.

2. Film and Animation: Streamlining Production

AI accelerates production processes:

• Storyboarding: Tools like MidJourney create detailed storyboards in minutes, visualizing scenes before production begins.

• AI-Generated Actors: Tools like DeepBrain AI create virtual actors, reducing costs while expanding creative possibilities.

3. Gaming: Interactive and Evolving Narratives

Games are already pushing the boundaries of storytelling:

- AI allows for branching storylines that adapt to player choices.

- Example: An AI dungeon-crawling game generates unique levels and story arcs based on each player's style.

4. Audio Storytelling: Immersive Podcasts and Soundscapes

Generative AI enhances audio narratives:

- AI creates lifelike voiceovers for audiobooks, ensuring accessibility.

- Tools like ElevenLabs generate custom soundscapes, from bustling markets to serene forests.

Advanced Applications of AI in Storytelling

1. Real-Time Story Adaptation

Imagine a movie that changes based on the audience's reactions. With real-time data analysis, AI can adapt dialogue, pacing, or even plot points.

Zero to Hero: Unlocking Creativity with AI

- Example: A live theater performance where AI adjusts the script based on audience feedback.

2. Generative World-Building

AI creates expansive, detailed universes with consistent lore:

- Example: A fantasy series where AI-generated maps, languages, and histories enrich the story, allowing creators to focus on character development.

3. Hyper-Personalized Content

AI tailors stories to individual readers or viewers, creating a deeply immersive experience:

- A family-friendly version of a horror story adjusts the intensity of scares based on the audience's preferences.

Jonah's AI-Powered Short Film

Zero to Hero: Unlocking Creativity with AI

Jonah's sci-fi short film, Echoes of Tomorrow, exemplifies how AI empowers independent creators:

1. The Vision: Jonah dreamed of depicting a dystopian world where memories could be traded as currency.

2. The Process:

- Visual Development: MidJourney generated vivid concept art of futuristic cities and memory archives.

- Script Refinement: Sudowrite helped Jonah craft emotionally compelling dialogue.

- Soundscapes: ElevenLabs created immersive sound effects, from buzzing marketplaces to haunting memory exchanges.

3. The Outcome: Jonah's film won awards at multiple festivals, praised for its originality and high production value achieved on a modest budget.

Ethical Considerations in AI Storytelling

With great power comes great responsibility. As AI takes on a larger role in storytelling, ethical concerns arise:

1. Ownership and Authorship

- Who owns an AI-generated story? The creator, the AI company, or both?

- Creators must navigate copyright laws to protect their work.

2. Avoiding Bias

AI models can unintentionally replicate harmful stereotypes. Creators must critically review AI outputs to ensure inclusivity and fairness.

3. Balancing Automation with Creativity

While AI can handle repetitive tasks, the heart of storytelling remains human. Creators should use AI to enhance, not replace, their personal touch.

Zero to Hero: Unlocking Creativity with AI

Future Trends in AI Storytelling

1. Augmented Reality Storytelling

AI and AR will combine to create stories you can literally walk through:

- Example: Explore a city while uncovering an interactive murder mystery through your AR glasses.

2. Decentralized Storytelling Communities

Platforms will emerge where creators collaborate with AI and audiences to co-create narratives in real time.

3. Immersive Fan Engagement

Fans will actively contribute to story development, voting on plot points or creating spin-off content with AI assistance.

Interactive Challenge: Create a Multi-Medium Story

Zero to Hero: Unlocking Creativity with AI

Expand your storytelling skills by creating a narrative across two or more mediums:

1. Start with an Idea: Choose a core concept for your story.

2. Develop the Mediums: Use AI to write a short story, create visuals for a comic, or script an audio drama.

3. Connect the Dots: Ensure the narrative flows seamlessly between mediums, creating a unified experience.

Reflect on how AI helped shape your multi-medium project and what challenges you encountered.

Notes Section

Reflect on your storytelling journey. Use these prompts to guide your thoughts:

1. How could you use AI to tell stories in new and innovative ways?

2. What medium excites you the most for AI-driven storytelling?

3. Write down three goals for your next storytelling project using AI.

Closing Reflection

Storytelling is evolving, and you're at the forefront of this transformation. With generative AI as your collaborator, you have the tools to create narratives that inspire, engage, and transcend boundaries. Your hero's journey as a storyteller is just beginning, and the possibilities are limitless. In the next chapter, we'll explore how AI is reshaping content creation for the metaverse, the next frontier of creativity.

Zero to Hero: Unlocking Creativity with AI

Chapter 13: Creating for the Metaverse

The Hero's Next Frontier: Shaping the Metaverse

In the hero's journey, every new chapter brings greater challenges and opportunities. Today, creators stand at the edge of the metaverse—a boundless digital universe where imagination becomes reality. With generative AI as your ally, the tools to shape this frontier are at your fingertips.

The metaverse is more than virtual reality or NFTs—it's a collaborative space where creators, communities, and economies converge. Whether you want to build immersive worlds, design collectible digital assets, or host unique experiences, AI can help

Zero to Hero: Unlocking Creativity with AI

you bring your ideas to life with unprecedented speed and creativity.

In this chapter, we'll dive deeper into how generative AI empowers creators to innovate in the metaverse, overcome challenges, and contribute to the evolution of this ever-expanding digital realm.

What is the Metaverse?

The metaverse can be thought of as the internet's next phase: a 3D, immersive, and interconnected space where users interact, create, and trade in real-time. Here are its defining features:

1. Interactivity: Users explore, create, and socialize within shared digital worlds.

2. Ownership: Blockchain technology allows users to own virtual assets, from real estate to fashion.

3. Persistence: Unlike traditional games or websites, the metaverse is always active, constantly evolving.

4. Interoperability: In the future, metaverse platforms will be seamlessly connected, allowing users to move their assets and identities across different worlds.

How AI Powers the Metaverse

Generative AI is revolutionizing metaverse creation by providing tools that streamline processes, spark innovation, and enhance user experiences.

1. World-Building Made Easy

AI automates the design of intricate landscapes, buildings, and environments:

- Example: NVIDIA Omniverse allows creators to collaboratively design lifelike virtual cities in real-time, complete with AI-simulated traffic, weather, and lighting.

2. Personalized Avatars and Fashion

AI generates hyper-realistic avatars and customizable outfits:

- Platforms like Ready Player Me and Zepeto use AI to create unique avatars that can be transported across metaverse platforms.

- Virtual Fashion: AI helps design everything from sneakers to couture gowns for avatars, allowing creators to sell unique items in digital marketplaces.

3. NFT Design and Deployment

NFTs are the metaverse's currency, representing ownership of digital assets. AI simplifies their creation and management:

- Use DALL·E or Artbreeder to generate stunning visuals for NFTs.

- AI tools like OpenAI Codex help write secure smart contracts for NFT transactions.

4. Intelligent NPCs and Experiences

AI powers interactive non-playable characters (NPCs) that enhance immersion:

- Example: In a virtual medieval town, an AI-driven NPC might act as a blacksmith, responding to players' needs and evolving based on interactions.

Mia's Virtual Art Empire

Mia, a traditional artist, had always dreamed of reaching a global audience. When she learned about the metaverse, she saw an opportunity to transform her art into a global phenomenon. Here's how she used generative AI to build her virtual art empire:

Step 1: Concept and Design

Mia used generative AI tools to design a virtual gallery that reflected her artistic style—abstract yet inviting.

- She leveraged MidJourney to create architectural concepts, combining surrealist curves with interactive spaces where visitors could "step into" her artwork.

Step 2: NFT Creation

Zero to Hero: Unlocking Creativity with AI

Using DALL·E, Mia generated digital art pieces inspired by her traditional work. She then added personal touches with Procreate before minting them as NFTs on platforms like OpenSea.

Step 3: Interactive Experiences

To make her gallery unique, Mia introduced AI-powered NPC guides that narrated the stories behind each piece. Visitors could interact with these guides, ask questions, and even commission personalized artwork.

Step 4: Overcoming Challenges

Mia faced several hurdles:

- Technical Knowledge: She initially struggled with blockchain and NFT platforms but used AI tutorials to learn quickly.

- Market Competition: By creating limited-edition NFTs with unique generative traits (e.g., changing colors based on the time of day), Mia stood out from other artists.

Zero to Hero: Unlocking Creativity with AI

The Outcome

Within a year, Mia had sold over $200,000 worth of NFTs and collaborated with brands to create metaverse-exclusive art installations. Her gallery became a hub for art enthusiasts, collectors, and collaborators.

Monetizing Creativity in the Metaverse

Generative AI opens the door to various income streams in the metaverse:

1. Virtual Goods and Collectibles

Creators can design and sell virtual items, from furniture to vehicles:

- Example: A designer uses AI to create modular virtual homes, allowing users to customize layouts and interiors.

2. Hosting Virtual Events

The metaverse thrives on unique experiences, such as concerts, workshops, or themed parties:

- AI-generated environments can adapt dynamically to audience feedback, ensuring every event feels tailored.

3. Offering Custom Services

Creators can provide bespoke services, like designing personalized avatars or virtual spaces for businesses.

Challenges and Ethical Considerations

Creating for the metaverse is not without its challenges:

1. Accessibility:

- While AI tools democratize creation, the cost of AR/VR hardware remains a barrier.

2. Sustainability:

- Blockchain's energy consumption raises concerns. Solutions like proof-of-stake and carbon offsets are critical.

3. Intellectual Property:

- Who owns an AI-generated asset? This remains a gray area requiring clear guidelines.

4. Inclusion:

- Ensuring that metaverse spaces are accessible and welcoming to all demographics is essential for its long-term success.

Future Trends in the Metaverse

1. AI-Enhanced Collaboration:

- Creators worldwide will collaborate in real-time using generative AI tools, bridging language and skill gaps.

2. Decentralized Economies:

- AI will optimize decentralized finance (DeFi) systems, enabling seamless trading and revenue-sharing models within the metaverse.

3. Hyper-Realistic Immersion:

Zero to Hero: Unlocking Creativity with AI

- Advanced AI will power photorealistic avatars, environments, and simulations, blurring the line between virtual and physical worlds.

Interactive Challenge: Build Your Metaverse Dream Project

Follow these steps to create something extraordinary in the metaverse:

1. Choose Your Focus: Will you design a virtual space, create NFTs, or host an event?

2. Use AI Tools: Experiment with platforms like DALL·E for visuals or ChatGPT for generating interactive scripts.

3. Launch and Share: Introduce your project to the metaverse community and gather feedback.

Reflect on the process and consider how you can improve or expand your project.

Zero to Hero: Unlocking Creativity with AI
Notes Section

Reflect on your creative ambitions in the metaverse. Use these prompts to guide your thoughts:

1. What excites you most about creating for the metaverse?

2. How can AI help you stand out in this growing space?

3. Write down three specific goals for your next metaverse project.

Zero to Hero: Unlocking Creativity with AI

Closing Reflection

The metaverse is a blank canvas, waiting for creators like you to bring it to life. With generative AI as your guide, the possibilities are limitless. Whether you're building worlds, designing assets, or crafting experiences, your contributions will shape this digital frontier. In the next chapter, we'll explore how AI can drive sustainability and inspire innovation for a better world.

Chapter 14: Monetizing Creativity: Proven Strategies for Success

The Hero's Reward: Turning Creativity into Income

For every creator, there comes a moment when passion meets purpose—when creativity transforms into a means to sustain and grow. This is the hero's reward, a culmination of learning, perseverance, and innovation. Generative AI offers creators a unique edge to unlock new revenue streams, reach broader audiences, and build sustainable careers.

In this expanded chapter, we'll explore diverse monetization strategies, real-world success stories, and actionable steps to turn your creative potential into tangible success. Whether you're starting small or aiming for a global audience, these strategies are designed to help you thrive.

Why Monetization Matters

For creators, monetization is about more than earning income. It represents:

1. Freedom: The ability to focus on creativity full-time without financial constraints.

2. Validation: Recognition of your skills, talents, and hard work.

3. Impact: Using earnings to amplify your message, reach more people, and inspire change.

The path to monetization isn't linear, but with generative AI as your ally, it's more accessible than ever.

Strategies to Monetize Your Creativity

1. Selling Digital Products

Digital products are one of the most versatile and scalable ways to monetize creativity:

Zero to Hero: Unlocking Creativity with AI

- What to Sell: E-books, templates, design packs, digital art, stock photos, music tracks, or video tutorials.

- How AI Helps: Use ChatGPT to draft e-books, Canva to design templates, and DALL·E to generate unique visuals.

Pro Tip: Offer "pay-what-you-want" pricing for your first few products to attract buyers and build trust.

2. Offering Freelance Services

Generative AI accelerates workflows, allowing you to offer high-quality services in less time:

- Examples:

- Writers: Use AI to create content outlines or edit drafts for blogs and articles.

- Designers: Generate concept art with MidJourney or create logos with Canva.

- Marketers: Craft ad campaigns or social media content using AI tools.

- Platforms: Fiverr, Upwork, Toptal, or even LinkedIn.

Pro Tip: Specialize in AI-enhanced services, such as "AI-powered copywriting" or "AI-driven branding," to stand out in a crowded market.

3. Creating and Selling NFTs

NFTs revolutionize how creators earn by enabling them to monetize digital art, collectibles, and experiences:

- What to Create:

- Unique digital art pieces.

- NFT series with themes, stories, or character collections.

- Interactive NFTs that evolve based on user interactions.

Zero to Hero: Unlocking Creativity with AI

- Tools: Use DALL·E for visuals, Blender for 3D models, and smart contract platforms like Mintbase.

Example: An artist designs an NFT collection featuring AI-generated characters, each with its own backstory. Buyers unlock exclusive content or future NFTs based on ownership.

Advanced Monetization Techniques

1. Subscription-Based Models

Create a recurring revenue stream by offering exclusive content or services:

- Examples:

- Monthly AI-generated design packs.

- Exclusive access to behind-the-scenes content or private webinars.

- Personalized AI tools or templates tailored to subscribers' needs.

- Platforms: Patreon, Substack, or your own website.

Pro Tip: Use generative AI to create bonus content that adds value for subscribers, like exclusive e-books or interactive challenges.

2. Licensing Your Work

Earn passive income by licensing your creations:

- What to License:

- AI-generated music for ads or films.

- Stock images for websites or publications.

- Design templates for brands or agencies.

- How to Start: Upload your work to platforms like Shutterstock, Adobe Stock, or Pond5.

Example: A photographer licenses AI-enhanced landscapes to travel blogs and earns royalties for every download.

Real-World Heroes of Monetization

1. Sam's AI-Powered Coaching Business

Sam, a graphic designer, faced stiff competition in his field. By leveraging generative AI, he turned his skills into a profitable coaching business:

1. Initial Strategy: Sam used AI to create personalized branding packages for small businesses.

2. Expansion: Clients began requesting workshops on using AI tools like Canva and MidJourney.

3. Results: Within a year, Sam's coaching business outpaced his design income, allowing him to scale.

2. Nina's NFT Ecosystem

Zero to Hero: Unlocking Creativity with AI

Nina, an independent artist, built a thriving NFT ecosystem:

1. Concept: Nina created an NFT series called "Future Worlds," featuring AI-generated art depicting futuristic cities.

2. Engagement: Each NFT owner received access to exclusive virtual tours of the cities, hosted in the metaverse.

3. Results: Nina's project earned over $500,000 and attracted collaboration offers from brands.

Overcoming Common Challenges

Monetizing creativity isn't without obstacles. Here's how to address them:

1. Building an Audience

- Use social media to showcase your work and engage with followers.

- Collaborate with other creators to expand your reach.

2. Pricing Your Work

- Research your niche and set competitive prices.

- Offer tiered pricing to cater to different budgets.

3. Staying Relevant

- Stay updated on trends in your industry.

- Experiment with new tools and platforms to keep your offerings fresh.

Emerging Trends in Monetization

1. Hybrid Products: Combining physical and digital creations (e.g., an art book paired with NFTs).

2. AI-Powered Marketplaces: Platforms designed for AI-generated content, offering creators dedicated spaces to showcase their work.

3. Interactive Experiences: Monetizing live, AI-driven experiences, like real-time story creation or virtual events.

Interactive Challenge: Monetize Your Passion

Take the following steps to create a monetization plan:

1. Identify Your Strengths: Choose a niche that aligns with your skills and interests.

2. Select a Strategy: Start with one method (e.g., selling digital products or offering services).

3. Launch and Iterate: Test your offerings with a small audience, gather feedback, and refine your approach.

Zero to Hero: Unlocking Creativity with AI

Reflect on your progress and consider expanding your strategy to diversify income streams.

Notes Section

Reflect on your monetization journey. Use these prompts to guide your thoughts:

1. What strengths can you leverage to create value?

2. How can you differentiate yourself in a competitive market?

3. Write down three goals for monetizing your creativity in the next six months.

Zero to Hero: Unlocking Creativity with AI

Closing Reflection

Zero to Hero: Unlocking Creativity with AI

Monetizing creativity isn't just about making money—it's about creating opportunities to grow, innovate, and inspire. With generative AI, you have the tools to turn your passion into a sustainable career. In the next chapter, we'll explore how AI is driving sustainability, helping creators innovate for a better world.

Chapter 15: AI and Sustainability: Innovating for a Better World

The Hero's Mission: Creating with Purpose

Every hero's journey includes a moment of reflection—a call to use their knowledge and tools for something greater than themselves. For creators, that moment is here. As the world grapples with environmental and societal challenges, sustainability has become a defining goal. Generative AI offers creators the opportunity to innovate responsibly, design with intention, and inspire change.

This chapter explores how AI-driven solutions can enhance sustainability, reduce waste, and foster collaboration. By integrating meaningful strategies and taking action, creators can align their work with the principles of eco-friendly innovation.

Why Sustainability Matters in Creativity

Zero to Hero: Unlocking Creativity with AI

Creativity has the power to shape perspectives and inspire action. By embedding sustainability into their work, creators contribute to three critical pillars:

1. Environmental Impact: Using resources wisely and minimizing waste.

2. Social Responsibility: Ensuring equity, accessibility, and ethical practices.

3. Economic Longevity: Building lasting systems that benefit people and the planet.

Generative AI amplifies these efforts, enabling creators to lead the charge toward a more sustainable future.

How AI Drives Sustainability

AI is already reshaping how we think about sustainability across industries:

1. Optimizing Resource Use

AI minimizes waste and maximizes efficiency:

- Example: In furniture design, AI tools like Rhino optimize material usage, generating cutting patterns that reduce offcuts.

2. Automating Sustainable Choices

AI tools analyze materials, processes, and energy consumption to recommend eco-friendly options:

- Example: Platforms like AutoDesk Fusion 360 help designers create lighter, stronger products with fewer resources.

3. Supporting Circular Economies

AI simplifies the reuse and recycling of materials:

- Example: In the fashion industry, AI-powered tools identify and repurpose textile waste for new garments.

4. Predicting Global Challenges

AI contributes to large-scale environmental initiatives:

- Example: Models like DeepMind are used to optimize renewable energy grids, while others predict deforestation patterns and track ocean pollution.

Real-World Impact

1. Olivia's Sustainable Packaging Revolution

Olivia, a graphic designer, transformed the packaging industry with generative AI.

- Problem: Most packaging was single-use and resource-intensive.

- Solution: Olivia used AI to design reusable and biodegradable packaging prototypes, reducing waste by 30%.

- Outcome: Her designs gained traction with major brands, leading to industry-wide adoption of greener practices.

Zero to Hero: Unlocking Creativity with AI

2. Ethan's Virtual Production Studio

Ethan, a filmmaker, faced high costs and waste from physical set construction.

- Solution: Using Unreal Engine and AI-driven tools like MidJourney, he created fully virtual sets.

- Outcome: His latest film was produced with 70% less physical material, setting a new standard for sustainability in the film industry.

Community-Driven Sustainability

Creators don't have to work alone. Generative AI fosters collaboration within sustainability-focused communities:

1. Collaborative Platforms

Tools like Miro and Hugging Face allow creators to crowdsource ideas for sustainable innovation.

- Example: A global team of architects co-designed an AI-optimized urban plan for energy-efficient housing.

2. Crowdsourcing Solutions

AI platforms aggregate input from diverse stakeholders to solve pressing problems:

- Example: A sustainability challenge on Kaggle resulted in an AI model that optimized irrigation systems, saving water in agriculture.

3. Empowering Local Action

Creators can use AI to adapt global solutions for local communities:

- Example: AI-generated designs for modular homes were customized to fit the needs of flood-prone regions in Southeast Asia.

Sustainability in Creative Fields

1. Fashion

Zero to Hero: Unlocking Creativity with AI

- Virtual Runways: Designers like The Fabricant use AI to create digital-only collections for the metaverse, eliminating physical waste.

- Circular Fashion: AI helps brands predict trends, ensuring they produce only what will sell.

2. Art and Entertainment

- Sustainable Installations: Digital art displayed in virtual galleries reduces the need for physical materials.

- Interactive Awareness Campaigns: AI-generated games educate players on sustainability issues.

3. Architecture and Urban Design

- Green Building: AI tools optimize energy efficiency and material selection for eco-friendly construction.

- Smart Cities: AI-driven urban planning reduces congestion, conserves energy, and improves public services.

Ethics of AI and Sustainability

With great power comes great responsibility. Here are key ethical considerations:

1. Energy Consumption

- Problem: Training large AI models requires significant energy.

- Solution: Use platforms committed to green AI practices, like Hugging Face's energy-efficient models.

2. Bias in AI Models

- Problem: AI may favor solutions that prioritize efficiency over equity.

- Solution: Creators should critically evaluate outputs to ensure inclusivity.

3. Transparency and Accountability

- Creators must disclose the tools and methods they use to ensure trust and ethical alignment.

Future Trends in Sustainable AI

1. Green AI Development

- The tech industry is focusing on smaller, energy-efficient models.

2. Personalized Sustainability

- AI will tailor eco-friendly solutions to individuals and businesses, making sustainability easier to adopt.

3. AI and Regenerative Design

- Future AI systems will go beyond minimizing harm to actively restoring ecosystems.

Interactive Challenge: Your Sustainable Impact

Zero to Hero: Unlocking Creativity with AI

Put your creativity to the test by designing an eco-friendly project with AI:

1. Choose a medium—fashion, architecture, art, or product design.

2. Use AI tools to minimize waste, improve efficiency, or innovate with sustainable materials.

3. Share your work with a sustainability-focused community to inspire others.

Reflect on how this project aligns with your goals and what you learned about balancing creativity and responsibility.

Reflect on how you can contribute to sustainability through creativity. Use these prompts:

1. What challenges in your creative process could AI help solve sustainably?

2. How can you use your platform to advocate for sustainability?

3. Write down three sustainability goals for your next year of creative work.

Closing Reflection

The hero's journey doesn't end with personal success—it continues with a mission to leave the world better than you found it. Generative AI provides the tools to innovate responsibly, reduce waste, and inspire sustainable practices. Your work has the power to create ripple effects, shaping a future where creativity and sustainability thrive together.

Zero to Hero: Unlocking Creativity with AI

In the next chapter, we'll explore how collaboration—blending human creativity, AI innovation, and collective effort—can unlock even greater possibilities.

Chapter 16: Collaborative Creativity: Teaming Up with AI and Humans

The Hero's Team: Strength in Collaboration

No hero achieves greatness alone. Allies and mentors are essential for overcoming obstacles, and in today's creative world, AI has emerged as one of the most powerful collaborators. But the real magic lies in the combined strength of human ingenuity and machine intelligence.

Collaboration, at its best, is about bringing together diverse talents and perspectives to achieve something greater than the sum of its parts. Generative AI introduces new possibilities to this dynamic, enabling creators to tackle complex challenges, bridge knowledge gaps, and innovate in ways previously unimaginable.

This chapter explores the evolving role of collaboration in creativity—between humans, AI,

Zero to Hero: Unlocking Creativity with AI

and global teams—and offers actionable insights for building partnerships that amplify results.

The Human-AI Dynamic: A New Era of Teamwork

The relationship between humans and AI can be seen as a partnership built on complementary strengths:

1. AI as the Catalyst: Generates ideas, analyzes data, and automates repetitive tasks.

2. Humans as the Heart: Add cultural relevance, emotional depth, and strategic direction.

This synergy not only enhances individual projects but also transforms how entire teams work together.

Example: A Multidisciplinary Design Team

Imagine a team tasked with reimagining urban spaces. AI creates data-driven models of energy-efficient layouts, while human architects add creative flair and cultural elements. The result is a city design that's both functional and inspiring.

Expanding Possibilities with AI Collaboration

1. Co-Creation in Real Time

AI tools enable teams to iterate faster than ever:

- Example: In a video game design studio, AI generates multiple level designs based on player feedback, allowing developers to test and refine ideas in hours instead of weeks.

2. Bridging Knowledge Gaps

AI empowers teams by filling in areas where expertise may be lacking:

- Example: A nonprofit uses AI to analyze environmental data and create compelling visuals for their awareness campaign, even without an in-house data scientist.

3. Automating Mundane Tasks

Zero to Hero: Unlocking Creativity with AI

Freeing up time for innovation:

- Example: Writers use AI to summarize research papers or draft outlines, focusing their energy on crafting engaging narratives.

Global Collaboration Through AI

When Lucas, a filmmaker in Brazil, wanted to create a documentary about climate change, he realized he needed input from experts around the world. With AI's help, Lucas assembled a virtual team:

1. Recruitment: AI algorithms identified climate scientists, photographers, and storytellers interested in the project.

2. Workflow: Team members uploaded their contributions to an AI-powered platform, which synthesized video footage, subtitles, and voiceovers.

3. Outcome: The documentary was completed in six months and premiered at an

Zero to Hero: Unlocking Creativity with AI

international film festival, showcasing perspectives from over 15 countries.

AI in Music Collaboration

A music producer in Tokyo teamed up with vocalists from different countries to create a multilingual pop album:

1. Concept: AI-generated beats and melodies were shared with singers, who added lyrics in their native languages.

2. Production: AI tools ensured seamless blending of different languages and styles.

3. Impact: The album became a hit on global streaming platforms, celebrated for its unique fusion of cultural influences.

Tools for Seamless Collaboration

1. For Creative Brainstorming

- Platform: ChatGPT, Jasper

- Use Case: Generate ideas for campaigns, character arcs, or brand slogans.

2. For Visual Collaboration

- Platform: Miro, Figma, Canva

- Use Case: Co-design layouts and visual assets in real time, with AI-enhanced suggestions.

3. For Workflow Management

- Platform: Notion, Monday.com, Trello

- Use Case: Assign tasks, track deadlines, and optimize resource allocation with AI-powered analytics.

Overcoming Challenges in AI Collaboration

1. Over Reliance on AI

- Risk: AI outputs may become repetitive or lack originality.

- Solution: Use AI as a starting point and refine outputs with human creativity.

  2. Bias and Ethics

- Risk: AI models may perpetuate biases in training data.

- Solution: Vet AI-generated content through diverse teams to ensure inclusivity.

  3. Resistance to AI

- Risk: Team members may feel intimidated by AI tools.

- Solution: Provide training and emphasize AI's supportive role.

The Future of Collaborative Creativity

1. AI-Powered Mediators: Imagine AI tools that facilitate brainstorming sessions by summarizing discussions and suggesting next steps.

2. Holographic Workspaces: Virtual environments where teams can meet, create, and prototype in 3D.

3. Dynamic Workflows: AI systems that adapt in real time, reallocating resources as project needs evolve.

Interactive Challenge: Collaborate Like a Hero

Create a project with a focus on teamwork and AI:

1. Define the Vision: Identify a goal that benefits from diverse perspectives and AI-enhanced efficiency.

2. Assemble Your Team: Include people with complementary skills and an AI platform tailored to the project.

3. Reflect and Iterate: After completing the project, discuss how AI influenced collaboration and how human input enriched the outcome.

Zero to Hero: Unlocking Creativity with AI
Notes Section

Reflect on how collaboration can elevate your projects. Use these prompts:

1. How can AI complement your strengths in a team setting?

2. What types of projects could benefit most from diverse, global collaboration?

3. Write down three ways you plan to integrate AI into your next team effort.

Zero to Hero: Unlocking Creativity with AI

Zero to Hero: Unlocking Creativity with AI

Closing Reflection

Collaboration is more than just working together—it's about building on each other's strengths to achieve something extraordinary. Generative AI transforms teamwork into a dynamic and limitless process, empowering creators to solve problems, share ideas, and innovate in ways never before possible.

In the next chapter, we'll explore how AI can uncover niche opportunities and monetize your creativity in underexplored markets.

Chapter 17: Monetizing Niche Opportunities with AI

The Hero's Hidden Treasure: Unlocking Niche Potential

In every hero's journey, there comes a moment of discovery—a hidden opportunity that transforms the ordinary into the extraordinary. For creative heroes exploring generative AI, this moment lies in identifying and monetizing niche opportunities. While many focus on mainstream markets, it's often the overlooked niches that hold the greatest potential for innovation, impact, and financial success.

This chapter dives deeper into the untapped potential of niche markets, offering real-world examples, actionable strategies, and practical tools to help you identify, create, and thrive in these specialized areas.

Why Niche Markets Matter

Zero to Hero: Unlocking Creativity with AI

Niche markets are like uncharted territories—smaller in scale but rich with opportunities:

1. Focused Attention: Niche audiences are highly engaged and willing to pay a premium for personalized solutions.

2. Room to Innovate: Smaller markets often lack tailored solutions, making them ripe for creative disruption.

3. Sustainable Growth: A loyal niche audience can provide consistent, long-term income streams.

AI-Powered Wedding Vows

Lila, a freelance writer, discovered that couples often struggled to express their feelings in wedding vows. She used generative AI to create a service that crafted personalized vows, speeches, and even wedding hashtags. By targeting this highly specific audience, Lila turned her side hustle into a six-figure business within two years.

Zero to Hero: Unlocking Creativity with AI

Identifying Your Unique Niche

Discovering a profitable niche involves a mix of self-reflection, market analysis, and creativity:

1. Tap into Your Passions

Your interests can guide you toward niches where your knowledge and enthusiasm shine:

- Example: A gardening enthusiast creates an AI-powered tool for planning sustainable backyard gardens based on climate data.

2. Explore Emerging Trends

Stay ahead of the curve by identifying industries where AI is gaining traction:

- Example: AI-driven wellness apps are revolutionizing personal fitness, offering tailored meal plans and workout routines.

3. Solve an Overlooked Problem

Zero to Hero: Unlocking Creativity with AI

Focus on specific challenges that mainstream solutions ignore:

- Example: AI-generated audio descriptions for visually impaired users make digital content more accessible.

Expanding Niche Market Opportunities

1. Hyper-Personalized Products

AI enables creators to offer deeply personalized services and products:

- Example: An artist uses AI to design custom comic books starring a client's family members as superheroes.

2. Regional and Cultural Adaptation

Localized content resonates deeply with specific audiences:

- Example: A content creator leverages AI to translate children's books into indigenous languages, preserving cultural heritage.

3. Sustainable Solutions

Eco-conscious consumers are drawn to innovative products that align with their values:

- Example: An entrepreneur uses AI to design reusable packaging tailored to niche markets like artisanal soap makers.

4. Educational Niches

AI tools can transform learning experiences for underserved communities:

- Example: A teacher creates AI-powered language tutorials for minority dialects, preserving linguistic diversity.

Reviving Vintage Fashion with AI

Jasmine, a fashion enthusiast, saw potential in the growing interest in vintage clothing. She used generative AI to design digital replicas of iconic outfits from past decades:

Zero to Hero: Unlocking Creativity with AI

1. The Concept: Jasmine combined AI-generated designs with her knowledge of fashion history.

2. The Execution: She sold the designs as NFTs and partnered with manufacturers to create limited-edition collections.

3. The Result: Jasmine built a loyal following of vintage fashion lovers, turning her passion into a profitable venture.

How to Monetize Your Niche

1. Create a Subscription Service

Offer ongoing value to your audience:

- Example: A subscription box service powered by AI curates monthly book recommendations based on readers' preferences.

2. Sell Digital Products

AI makes it easy to create templates, guides, and other downloadable assets:

- Example: A designer sells AI-generated patterns for sewing enthusiasts, catering to a niche community of hobbyists.

3. Partner with Influencers

Collaborate with niche influencers to amplify your reach:

- Example: An AI tool for creating custom pet portraits partners with pet influencers to showcase its offerings.

Overcoming Challenges in Niche Monetization

1. Building Trust

Customers in niche markets value authenticity. Be transparent about your use of AI and focus on delivering quality.

- Example: A personalized skincare brand shares insights into how their AI recommendations are developed, building customer confidence.

2. Navigating Smaller Audiences

Smaller audiences require creative marketing strategies:

• Solution: Use targeted ads and leverage community-driven platforms like Reddit or niche forums.

3. Adapting to Feedback

Niche markets evolve quickly. Regularly update your offerings based on customer feedback and industry trends.

Future Trends in Niche Opportunities

1. AI-Powered Microbusinesses: Creators will use AI to run highly specialized, one-person businesses serving niche audiences.

2. Collaborative Ecosystems: Niche creators will team up, sharing resources and expertise to address interconnected markets.

3. Smart Niche Matching: AI platforms will emerge to connect creators with underserved niches based on their skills and interests.

Interactive Challenge: Define Your Niche Path

Take actionable steps toward building your AI-powered niche business:

1. Identify a Problem: What specific challenge can you solve for a niche audience?

2. Test Your Idea: Use generative AI to create a prototype or mockup of your solution.

3. Engage Your Audience: Reach out to potential customers through surveys or social media to refine your offering.

Notes Section

Reflect on how you can turn your passions into a thriving niche business. Use these prompts:

1. What hobbies or interests could inspire a unique product or service?

2. How can AI help you personalize or scale your offerings?

3. Write down three niche ideas and outline the steps to bring them to life.

Closing Reflection

Niche opportunities are the hidden treasures of the creative world. By blending your unique skills

Zero to Hero: Unlocking Creativity with AI

with the power of generative AI, you can uncover markets that are both impactful and lucrative. The key is to remain curious, innovative, and committed to delivering real value.

In the next chapter, we'll explore how gamification can transform your creative journey into an engaging, rewarding adventure.

Chapter 18: Gamifying Your Creative Journey

The Hero's Game: Turning Challenges into Achievements

Every hero's journey features challenges that, once overcome, become transformative milestones. These moments not only measure progress but also fuel the hero's motivation to continue. In your creative journey with generative AI, gamification can serve as a powerful tool to replicate this dynamic—transforming tasks into rewarding, engaging experiences.

Gamification is more than just a productivity hack. It's a way to make your journey enjoyable and immersive, turning the creative process into a game worth playing. This chapter dives deeper into how gamification works, how generative AI enhances it, and how you can integrate it into your workflow for maximum impact.

The Science of Gamification

Gamification works because it aligns with how our brains process motivation and reward:

1. Progress Visibility: Seeing tangible milestones makes long-term goals feel achievable.

2. Dopamine Rewards: Completing tasks triggers a sense of achievement, driving you to continue.

3. Intrinsic Motivation: Playful challenges encourage exploration and experimentation without fear of failure.

For instance, Emma, a freelance graphic designer, struggled to maintain focus during long projects. Inspired by video games, she gamified her workflow. Using AI tools like Figma's design assistant, she set daily quests—small, achievable goals with rewards like extra free time or new design brushes. Within three months, Emma's productivity soared, and she felt more connected to her work.

Zero to Hero: Unlocking Creativity with AI

Gamification Techniques for Everyday Creativity

1. The Creative Level-Up System

Turn your skills into a progression system where each milestone unlocks new abilities or tools:

- Example: Earn "levels" by mastering new AI platforms. Reach "Level 10" by publishing your first AI-assisted project.

2. Achievement Badges

Create visual markers for accomplishments to celebrate progress:

- Example: Design custom badges like "Prompt Master" for crafting effective AI prompts or "Visual Virtuoso" for generating unique AI art.

3. Dynamic Leaderboards

Compete with yourself or a team by tracking progress and achievements:

- Example: Use Monday.com to compare project milestones across team members, encouraging friendly competition.

4. Randomized Challenges

Introduce unpredictability to keep things fresh:

- Example: Ask ChatGPT to generate a random creative challenge each week, such as designing a product logo for an imaginary company.

AI-Enhanced Gamification Tools

Generative AI can amplify the effects of gamification by providing tailored feedback, challenges, and rewards:

1. Personalized Daily Challenges

Platforms like ChatGPT and Jasper can create custom daily prompts and tasks:

- Example: Start each morning with an AI-generated list of creative exercises aligned with your goals.

Zero to Hero: Unlocking Creativity with AI

2. Smart Progress Tracking

AI-powered tools analyze your workflow and suggest areas for improvement:

- Example: Use tools like Descript or Grammarly to measure progress and set improvement goals for writing or editing projects.

3. AI-Driven Feedback Loops

Get immediate, actionable feedback to refine your work:

- Example: Let MidJourney critique and iterate on your visual designs based on user feedback.

Gamification in Team Settings

When a marketing agency struggled to stay motivated during a major product campaign, they turned to gamification for a creative boost. The team divided tasks into "quests" on a shared digital board. Each completed quest—whether a new ad concept, social media visual, or email draft—earned points toward a collective team reward.

The result? Productivity spiked, team morale improved, and the client received a campaign that surpassed expectations.

Collaborative gamification doesn't just add fun to projects—it builds camaraderie and a sense of shared purpose. By integrating AI tools for task generation, feedback, and performance tracking, teams can streamline workflows while keeping motivation high.

Expanding the Interactive Challenge

Interactive Challenge: Gamify Your Workflow

Turn your current project into a gamified adventure:

1. Set Up Your Game: Define goals, milestones, and rules. For example, completing a draft could earn you points, while revisions unlock new rewards.

Zero to Hero: Unlocking Creativity with AI

2. Use AI for Support: Incorporate tools like Canva for visual tasks, Jasper for writing, or Miro for brainstorming.

3. Create Rewards: Identify meaningful incentives—like a creative workshop or a day off—for reaching key milestones.

Ideas for Specific Industries:

- Content Creators: Gamify scriptwriting with AI-generated scene prompts and rewards for completing drafts.

- Artists: Challenge yourself to create a themed collection, with each piece building toward a final showcase.

- Educators: Develop interactive lesson plans, using AI to generate unique challenges for students.

Future Trends in Gamified Creativity

Zero to Hero: Unlocking Creativity with AI

1. AI-Generated Game Worlds: Imagine virtual workspaces where tasks are visualized as quests in a fantasy setting.

2. Adaptive Gamification Models: AI will customize games to fit your unique workflow, adjusting challenges and rewards in real time.

3. Immersive VR Experiences: Gamification will evolve into interactive VR environments, turning creative work into a fully engaging experience.

Notes Section

Reflect on how gamification can enhance your creative process. Use these prompts:

1. How can you incorporate gamification into your daily workflow?

2. What rewards or incentives motivate you most?

Zero to Hero: Unlocking Creativity with AI

3. Write down three gamified project ideas and outline how you'll bring them to life.

Zero to Hero: Unlocking Creativity with AI

Closing Reflection

Gamification transforms creativity into an adventure filled with challenges, rewards, and growth. By integrating generative AI into your gamification strategy, you'll unlock new levels of productivity, engagement, and joy in your work.

In the next chapter, we'll explore hyper-personalization and how AI can tailor content, products, and experiences to meet individual needs, unlocking even greater creative potential.

Chapter 19: AI and Hyper-Personalization

The Hero's Connection: Crafting Uniquely Tailored Experiences

Imagine standing in front of a bookshelf where every book has been written with you in mind. Each story speaks directly to your dreams, preferences, and goals. This is the promise of hyper-personalization—an experience so tailored that it feels uniquely yours. For the creative hero, hyper-personalization powered by generative AI isn't just a tool; it's a transformative ally in creating meaningful connections.

This chapter dives into the mechanics, applications, and ethical considerations of hyper-personalization, showing you how to harness AI to deliver experiences that resonate deeply with individuals and communities alike.

Zero to Hero: Unlocking Creativity with AI

What is Hyper-Personalization?

Hyper-personalization is more than adding a name to an email or offering a handful of pre-set choices. It's the art of using data, behavior analysis, and AI-driven insights to craft experiences tailored to the unique needs and desires of each individual.

A Simple Analogy:

• Customization: Choosing the toppings on your pizza.

• Personalization: The chef knowing your favorite toppings, the precise ratio of cheese to sauce, and offering it before you ask.

AI makes this possible by processing vast amounts of information and generating tailored outputs in real time. Whether you're an artist, entrepreneur, or educator, this ability to connect on a deeply personal level opens up a world of opportunities.

How AI Powers Hyper-Personalization

Zero to Hero: Unlocking Creativity with AI

Generative AI enables hyper-personalization by combining creativity with data-driven insights:

1. Data Collection and Analysis: AI gathers and interprets user preferences, feedback, and behaviors.

2. Real-Time Adaptation: AI tools adjust content dynamically based on new information.

3. Creative Generation: AI produces tailored outputs—whether text, visuals, or experiences—that align with individual needs.

Example: The Personalized Story Engine

A children's storytelling app uses AI to craft bedtime tales featuring each child as the hero. Parents input details like favorite animals, hobbies, and friends' names, and the app weaves these elements into personalized narratives. Children light up as they see themselves reflected in the story, building emotional connections and encouraging creativity.

Hyper-Personalization in Action

1. Tailored Content Creation

AI empowers creators to deliver content that feels intimate and relevant:

- Writers: Imagine newsletters that adjust tone, depth, and topic based on individual reader preferences.

- Artists: Combine tools like MidJourney with client input to produce bespoke art pieces.

- Marketers: Design AI-driven campaigns where every email, ad, and landing page adapts to user data in real time.

2. Personalized Education

Learning paths tailored to each student's pace and preferences make education more effective:

- Example: A language-learning app adapts vocabulary lessons based on what users struggle with, reinforcing weak areas while building confidence.

3. Bespoke Shopping Experiences

E-commerce platforms use AI to deliver curated product recommendations:

- Example: An AI-powered clothing store offers personalized outfit suggestions based on the customer's style history, body measurements, and upcoming events.

Real-World Impact: Hyper-Personalization in Business

Mia, the owner of a small online boutique, felt overshadowed by larger competitors. She turned to generative AI to create a hyper-personalized shopping experience:

Zero to Hero: Unlocking Creativity with AI

1. Dynamic Recommendations: AI analyzed each customer's browsing and purchase history to suggest products tailored to their tastes.

2. Engaging Outreach: AI-generated newsletters offered style tips and exclusive discounts personalized to each subscriber's preferences.

3. Interactive Features: A virtual stylist quiz designed by AI helped customers discover their "style persona," deepening engagement.

The results were remarkable. Within a year, repeat purchases increased by 50%, and Mia's customers praised the boutique for its "thoughtful, personal touch."

Expanding Opportunities with Hyper-Personalization

1. Health and Wellness

AI can create highly personalized plans for fitness, nutrition, and mental health:

Zero to Hero: Unlocking Creativity with AI

- Example: A fitness app analyzes daily activity levels, preferences, and goals to offer customized workout routines and meal suggestions.

2. Entertainment

Streaming platforms are leveraging AI to curate hyper-specific recommendations:

- Example: Personalized playlists that adapt to the listener's mood, time of day, or social context.

3. Travel Experiences

Hyper-personalization elevates travel planning to a new level:

- Example: An AI travel assistant crafts itineraries tailored to a traveler's interests, dietary restrictions, and preferred pace.

The Ethics of Hyper-Personalization

With great personalization comes great responsibility. As creators and businesses leverage

AI, it's essential to navigate the ethical considerations:

1. Transparency: Make it clear when and how AI is tailoring experiences.

2. Privacy: Respect user data and avoid collecting unnecessary information.

3. Avoid Manipulation: Ensure hyper-personalization serves the user's needs, not just business goals.

Thoughtful Design

Consider a wellness app that offers personalized stress-management strategies. While effective, the app must clearly explain how user data is used and avoid promoting unnecessary products under the guise of personalization.

Future Trends in Hyper-Personalization

Zero to Hero: Unlocking Creativity with AI

1. Emotionally Intelligent AI: Tools that adapt based on users' emotional cues, such as voice tone or facial expressions.

2. Virtual Reality Personalization: VR spaces customized to the user's preferences, creating immersive, personalized experiences.

3. Cultural Adaptation: AI systems that tailor experiences to reflect the cultural and linguistic nuances of different regions.

Interactive Challenge: Personalize Your Project

Apply hyper-personalization to your creative or professional endeavors:

1. Define Your Audience: Choose a specific individual or group to target.

2. Leverage AI Tools: Use generative AI to create tailored content, such as custom illustrations, marketing copy, or interactive experiences.

3. Test and Iterate: Share your personalized creation, gather feedback, and refine it for greater impact.

Notes Section

Reflect on how hyper-personalization can elevate your work. Use these prompts:

1. What creative projects could benefit from AI-powered tailoring?

2. How can you gather meaningful data to improve personalization?

3. Outline one hyper-personalized idea and the steps needed to execute it.

Zero to Hero: Unlocking Creativity with AI

Closing Reflection

Hyper-personalization is a transformative force, enabling creators to connect deeply with audiences and customers. By embracing generative AI, you can craft experiences that feel truly unique, building trust, loyalty, and lasting impact.

Zero to Hero: Unlocking Creativity with AI

In the next chapter, we'll explore how to stay ahead of AI's rapid evolution—adapting your creativity to the technologies of tomorrow.

Chapter 20: Adapting to AI's Evolution

The Hero's Adaptation: Thriving in a Changing Landscape

Every hero's journey reaches a point where adaptation becomes essential. Whether it's learning a new skill, embracing a mentor's guidance, or recalibrating a mission, growth depends on the ability to evolve. In the ever-changing landscape of AI, the same holds true. The tools and trends you rely on today may be unrecognizable tomorrow, replaced by innovations that require new approaches and strategies.

To thrive, the creative hero must embrace adaptability—not as a burden but as a skill that unlocks new opportunities. This chapter explores how to navigate AI's rapid evolution, turn challenges into growth, and ensure your creative journey remains vibrant and forward-focused.

Zero to Hero: Unlocking Creativity with AI

Why Adapting to AI is Essential

Generative AI is evolving at an exponential rate. New tools are introduced almost daily, while existing platforms undergo updates that expand their capabilities. Adaptability ensures that you remain agile, ready to embrace change and integrate emerging technologies into your work.

Key benefits of adaptability include:

1. Resilience: Navigating shifts without losing momentum.

2. Innovation: Leveraging new tools and methods to stay ahead of the curve.

3. Sustainability: Building skills and workflows that withstand technological shifts.

Emerging Trends in Generative AI

To adapt effectively, it's crucial to understand the trends shaping AI's future. Here's what to watch:

1. Multi-Modal AI

Zero to Hero: Unlocking Creativity with AI

Multi-modal systems are breaking boundaries by seamlessly integrating text, images, audio, and video.

- Example: Tools like Adobe Firefly allow users to combine textual prompts with visual enhancements, creating interactive content.

2. AI-Driven Collaboration

AI tools are evolving from passive assistants to active collaborators, offering feedback and co-creation capabilities.

- Example: A writer uses AI to suggest alternate endings for a story, enriching the narrative with diverse perspectives.

3. Ethical AI Development

As AI grows more powerful, ethical concerns around transparency, fairness, and accountability will shape its development.

- Example: Platforms now include features to explain their decision-making processes, fostering trust among users.

4. Personalized AI Systems

AI will increasingly adapt to individual workflows, offering tailored interfaces and suggestions.

- Example: A personalized AI dashboard that prioritizes tools and tasks based on your creative habits.

Strategies for Staying Ahead

1. Lifelong Learning

Commit to continuous education to keep up with evolving AI tools:

- Example: Attend webinars, follow AI experts on social media, or explore advanced courses on platforms like Coursera.

2. Experimentation

Zero to Hero: Unlocking Creativity with AI

Approach new tools with curiosity and a willingness to fail:

- Example: Try using a beta version of an AI program for a small project to familiarize yourself with its features.

3. Flexible Workflows

Design adaptable processes that allow you to integrate new tools seamlessly:

- Example: Use cloud-based software that updates automatically and connects with multiple AI platforms.

4. Collaborative Learning

Join communities of like-minded creators to share insights and discover emerging trends:

- Example: Participate in AI forums, attend hackathons, or create a mastermind group focused on generative tools.

Skills Every Creative Hero Needs

Zero to Hero: Unlocking Creativity with AI

To adapt successfully, hone these essential skills:

1. Curiosity: Stay excited about exploring new possibilities.

2. Critical Thinking: Evaluate tools to determine their impact on your workflow.

3. Resilience: Overcome setbacks and view challenges as opportunities.

Real-World Story: Turning Challenges into Growth

Lucas, a motion designer, faced an unexpected hurdle when his favorite animation software was discontinued. Instead of resisting change, Lucas leaned into the unknown. He explored AI-driven alternatives, discovering tools that automated repetitive tasks like frame interpolation. This shift allowed Lucas to focus on storytelling, a skill that elevated his work and attracted new clients.

Lucas's adaptability turned what could have been a career setback into a transformative leap forward.

Team Success Through Adaptation

When a marketing agency began integrating AI, initial resistance threatened to stall progress. To encourage buy-in, the agency leaders gamified the process, awarding team members for experimenting with new tools like ChatGPT and MidJourney. Within weeks, the team was generating AI-assisted ad campaigns with impressive results.

By embracing change as a team, they not only improved productivity but also fostered a culture of innovation.

Interactive Challenge: Your Adaptation Playbook

1. Identify an Emerging Tool: Research a cutting-edge AI platform or trend.

2. Create a Test Project: Apply the tool to a low-stakes project to explore its capabilities.

3. Document Your Insights: Write down what worked, what didn't, and how you can integrate the tool into future projects.

4. Share Your Findings: Present your learnings to peers or online communities, fostering collective growth.

Notes Section

Reflect on your adaptability and future strategies. Use these prompts:

1. What recent changes in your field required you to adapt?

2. How can you build resilience in the face of rapid technological shifts?

3. Outline one specific action you'll take to stay ahead in AI innovation.

Zero to Hero: Unlocking Creativity with AI

Closing Reflection

Adapting to AI's evolution isn't just about keeping up—it's about leading the way. With curiosity, flexibility, and a commitment to growth, you can turn the rapid pace of change into a source of inspiration and innovation.

In the next chapter, we'll explore how generative AI empowers entrepreneurs to disrupt industries, build unique value propositions, and forge their creative legacies.

Chapter 21: The Entrepreneur's Edge: AI-Powered Innovation

The Hero as Innovator: Embracing the Edge of Change

For every hero, there comes a moment when they must step out of their comfort zone and embrace bold innovation. In the entrepreneurial world, generative AI is the game-changing ally that enables this leap. It empowers creators and businesses to reimagine their industries, disrupt the status quo, and unlock entirely new opportunities.

AI isn't just a tool—it's an accelerator. For the entrepreneur, it's the catalyst that transforms ideas into action, enhances customer experiences, and fuels sustainable growth. In this chapter, we'll explore how entrepreneurs—whether aspiring or experienced—can use AI to drive innovation, solve problems, and build ventures that thrive in today's fast-paced landscape.

Zero to Hero: Unlocking Creativity with AI

Why AI is the Entrepreneur's Ultimate Advantage

Entrepreneurship is fundamentally about solving problems and creating value. Generative AI accelerates this process by:

1. Streamlining Workflows: AI automates repetitive tasks, freeing entrepreneurs to focus on strategy and creativity.

2. Unlocking Creativity: Generative AI provides fresh ideas and solutions, helping entrepreneurs innovate.

3. Scaling Fast: AI tools allow businesses to grow rapidly without proportional increases in resources.

The Competitive Edge

Entrepreneurs who adopt generative AI early gain a competitive edge by offering faster, more tailored solutions to customers. This advantage isn't limited to tech-savvy startups—businesses in industries like retail, hospitality, and wellness are also leveraging AI to differentiate themselves.

Take Sarah, for example, who launched a small online jewelry brand. Using AI, she designed unique collections, crafted personalized marketing campaigns, and managed customer interactions—all with a single toolset. Within eight months, Sarah's revenue tripled, and her brand became known for its innovative approach.

Key Areas Where Entrepreneurs Can Leverage AI

1. Product Development

AI helps entrepreneurs turn ideas into reality:

• Example: A fashion startup uses AI to design custom clothing patterns based on market trends.

• Example: An app developer integrates AI to generate dynamic user interfaces tailored to individual preferences.

AI can also accelerate prototyping, allowing businesses to test new ideas faster and more affordably. Tools like Canva Pro's design automation or ChatGPT's coding assistance enable entrepreneurs to create prototypes that look professional and perform effectively, even with minimal resources.

2. Marketing and Branding

AI tools craft data-driven campaigns and boost brand visibility:

• Example: Jasper generates personalized ad copy, while MidJourney creates unique visuals for social media.

• Example: Email marketing platforms like Klaviyo use AI to predict customer behavior and recommend optimized campaigns.

3. Customer Engagement

AI enhances the customer experience by providing personalized solutions:

Zero to Hero: Unlocking Creativity with AI

- Example: ChatGPT powers customer service bots that resolve queries efficiently.

- Example: AI tools create interactive product quizzes to guide customers toward the best purchases.

With the rise of conversational AI, businesses can also engage with their audiences in real time, offering tailored responses and actionable recommendations.

4. Operations and Logistics

Generative AI optimizes workflows and resource management:

- Example: AI-powered inventory systems predict stock needs and reduce waste.

- Example: AI streamlines HR processes, from candidate screening to onboarding materials.

Zero to Hero: Unlocking Creativity with AI

By automating routine tasks, entrepreneurs can dedicate more time to innovation and strategy, driving long-term success.

The Future of AI-Powered Entrepreneurship

As AI continues to evolve, the possibilities for entrepreneurial innovation expand:

1. AI-Driven Marketplaces

Platforms that use AI to connect creators, buyers, and collaborators will become more intelligent, offering personalized recommendations and fostering dynamic collaborations.

2. Automated Business Models

Companies increasingly rely on AI for decision-making, supply chain management, and even creative direction. Imagine businesses that operate 24/7 with minimal human intervention.

3. Predictive Business Development

Zero to Hero: Unlocking Creativity with AI

Future AI systems may analyze global trends and offer predictive insights into emerging markets or untapped customer needs, allowing entrepreneurs to act before their competitors.

4. AI-Driven Globalization

AI will simplify international trade and collaboration. Entrepreneurs will be able to localize products and services for new markets quickly, thanks to tools like language AI and cultural adaptation models.

5. Immersive Branding Experiences

AI will empower businesses to create personalized, interactive brand experiences using augmented reality (AR) and virtual reality (VR). Customers could "walk through" a virtual store designed just for them.

6. Niche Business Models

As AI tools become more accessible, micro-entrepreneurs will emerge with hyper-specific

Zero to Hero: Unlocking Creativity with AI

offerings. These businesses will use AI to address niche customer needs that larger companies might overlook.

Interactive Framework: The AI Innovation Cycle

1. Identify the Need: What problem are you solving? Use AI tools to research market gaps and customer pain points.

2. Ideate Solutions: Experiment with generative AI to brainstorm and prototype innovative ideas.

3. Test and Iterate: Deploy AI-powered simulations to refine your product or service.

4. Scale with AI: Use AI for targeted marketing, operational efficiency, and customer engagement as you grow.

Interactive Challenge: Innovate Boldly

Industry-Specific Prompts

Zero to Hero: Unlocking Creativity with AI

1. Fashion: Use AI to design a small collection of clothing inspired by an emerging cultural trend.

2. Education: Develop an interactive course module powered by AI that adapts to different learning styles.

3. Sustainability: Create a business model for a sustainable product using AI to optimize materials and processes.

4. Health and Wellness: Design a personalized wellness app feature, such as AI-generated fitness routines based on user preferences.

5. Hospitality: Develop a customer journey map for a boutique hotel that adapts to guest preferences using AI tools like ChatGPT and MidJourney.

For each prompt:

- Use at least one generative AI tool to bring your idea to life.

- Share your prototype or concept with peers or online communities for feedback.

Real-World Stories: Innovation in Action

Omar's Journey to Sustainability

Omar used AI to identify untapped markets, design eco-friendly prototypes, and streamline his supply chain. His ability to adapt allowed him to disrupt the market with a unique value proposition.

The Interactive Boutique

A small jewelry store used AI to create interactive digital fittings, allowing customers to "try on" pieces virtually. This innovative approach boosted conversions by 40% in six months.

Notes Section

Reflect on how AI can amplify your entrepreneurial journey. Use these prompts:

Zero to Hero: Unlocking Creativity with AI

1. What areas of your business or creative projects could benefit most from AI innovation?

2. How can AI help you scale without losing your personal touch?

3. Brainstorm one AI-driven idea you could implement this month.

Zero to Hero: Unlocking Creativity with AI

Closing Reflection

Generative AI is not just a tool—it's a partner in innovation, capable of turning bold ideas into transformative ventures. By leveraging its power, you can disrupt industries, solve meaningful problems, and create a legacy that reflects your unique vision.

In the next chapter, we'll explore how generative AI impacts health, fitness, and lifestyle—

Zero to Hero: Unlocking Creativity with AI reshaping personal well-being and everyday experiences.

Chapter 22: AI in Health, Fitness, and Lifestyle

The Hero's Personal Growth: Balancing Innovation and Well-Being

The hero's journey isn't just about external accomplishments; it's also about personal transformation. In the realm of health, fitness, and lifestyle, generative AI offers tools that empower individuals to prioritize well-being, foster balance, and achieve personal goals.

From meal planning and fitness routines to mental health support, AI is reshaping how we approach daily life. This chapter explores how you can leverage generative AI to enhance your physical, mental, and emotional health—ensuring that your journey to creativity and success is as fulfilling as it is transformative.

AI's Role in Personal Well-Being

Zero to Hero: Unlocking Creativity with AI

Generative AI's capacity to analyze patterns, personalize recommendations, and adapt in real time makes it a powerful ally for improving health and lifestyle. Here's how:

1. Personalization: Tailored fitness plans, diet recommendations, and mindfulness practices that align with your unique needs.

2. Accessibility: Tools that make expert-level advice and strategies available to anyone, anytime.

3. Consistency: AI-powered reminders and habit trackers help maintain momentum toward health goals.

Key Applications of AI in Health and Lifestyle

1. Fitness and Exercise

AI is transforming fitness by providing real-time feedback, personalized workouts, and immersive experiences:

- Example: Apps like Fitbod generate strength-training plans based on user performance and equipment availability.

- Example: AI-powered devices like Peloton offer dynamic workout programs and live feedback for maximum efficiency.

Imagine having a virtual personal trainer that learns your habits, adapts to your progress, and keeps you motivated with fresh routines.

2. Nutrition and Meal Planning

Generative AI simplifies healthy eating by creating meal plans tailored to your dietary preferences and goals:

- Example: Tools like EatLove generate weekly meal plans with recipes, shopping lists, and nutritional breakdowns.

- Example: AI assistants can suggest substitutes for ingredients, ensuring you maintain a balanced diet even with limited supplies.

Zero to Hero: Unlocking Creativity with AI

For those navigating dietary restrictions or busy schedules, AI becomes a game-changer for maintaining nutritional health.

3. Mental Health and Mindfulness

AI's impact on mental well-being is equally profound, offering support for stress management, mindfulness, and emotional resilience:

- Example: Meditation apps like Headspace use AI to create personalized meditation programs that adapt to your mood.

- Example: ChatGPT-powered tools provide conversational support for reflection and journaling, promoting mental clarity.

These tools don't replace professional care but can complement therapy, offering accessible support for everyday challenges.

4. Preventive Health and Wearables

Zero to Hero: Unlocking Creativity with AI

AI-driven wearable devices are redefining health monitoring by identifying risks early:

• Example: Fitbit and Apple Watch track heart rate, sleep patterns, and physical activity, offering tailored insights for long-term health.

• Future Trend: Predictive algorithms that detect signs of chronic illnesses before symptoms manifest, enabling proactive care.

Real-World Stories: Living Healthier with AI

Jessica's Fitness Journey

After years of struggling with a sedentary lifestyle, Jessica decided to make a change. She downloaded an AI-powered fitness app and began tracking her progress. The app provided workout recommendations tailored to her schedule and fitness level, along with a meal planner that accounted for her preferences and caloric needs.

Jessica's progress was slow but steady. Within six months, she had built a consistent routine, lost weight, and gained confidence. By combining generative AI tools with her determination, Jessica reclaimed her health and energy—proving that small steps lead to big transformations.

Alex's Mental Resilience

As a remote worker managing high stress levels, Alex turned to AI for support. Using a journaling app powered by ChatGPT, Alex developed a daily routine of reflecting on challenges and setting intentions. Over time, the app's feedback helped Alex identify patterns that triggered stress, leading to actionable strategies for balance.

With mindfulness prompts and stress-relief exercises generated by the app, Alex regained a sense of control over their mental well-being, illustrating the value of AI-driven self-care.

Future Innovations in AI for Health and Lifestyle

1. DNA-Based Wellness Plans

AI-powered health platforms will soon integrate genetic data to create ultra-personalized fitness and nutrition plans based on individual DNA profiles.

2. Smart Kitchens

AI-driven kitchen assistants will help users create recipes, track ingredients, and reduce food waste by suggesting meals based on available supplies.

3. Augmented Reality (AR) Fitness

AR will merge with AI to create immersive workout environments, such as virtual hiking trails or interactive yoga sessions with real-time adjustments.

4. Community Wellness Platforms

AI-powered platforms will facilitate group challenges, encouraging collective health goals and fostering community accountability.

Zero to Hero: Unlocking Creativity with AI

Interactive Challenge: Design Your AI-Enhanced Health Plan

7-Day AI Wellness Challenge

1. Day 1: Identify your primary health goal (e.g., fitness, mindfulness, nutrition).

2. Day 2: Research an AI tool or app to support your goal (e.g., Fitbod, EatLove, Headspace).

3. Day 3: Set a measurable milestone for the week (e.g., a specific number of workouts or journal entries).

4. Day 4: Implement the tool and document your experience.

5. Day 5: Reflect on challenges and adjust your approach.

6. Day 6: Share your progress with a peer or online community for feedback.

7. Day 7: Evaluate your results and plan your next steps.

By engaging with this challenge, you'll experience firsthand how AI can enhance your well-being and establish sustainable habits.

Notes Section

Reflect on how AI can enhance your health and lifestyle. Use these prompts:

1. What health challenges could AI help you address?

2. How can AI tools make your routine more consistent and enjoyable?

3. Write down one actionable step you'll take this week to improve your well-being.

Zero to Hero: Unlocking Creativity with AI

Zero to Hero: Unlocking Creativity with AI

Closing Reflection

Generative AI is more than a tool for productivity—it's a partner in personal growth. By embracing AI in health, fitness, and lifestyle, you can unlock the energy and balance needed to sustain your creative journey.

In the next chapter, we'll explore how generative AI empowers entrepreneurs to disrupt industries, build unique value propositions, and forge their creative legacies.

Zero to Hero: Unlocking Creativity with AI

Chapter 23: Exploring New Markets with AI

The Hero's Quest: Seeking Hidden Opportunities

Every hero faces a moment of discovery—an opportunity to venture into the unknown and uncover untapped potential. For entrepreneurs, creators, and innovators, generative AI opens doors to markets and opportunities that were previously invisible or inaccessible.

This chapter is your guide to navigating the uncharted. You'll learn how to identify new markets, use AI tools to analyze trends, and position yourself as a pioneer in emerging spaces. By the end, you'll not only know where the opportunities lie but also how to seize them with confidence.

The Role of AI in Market Exploration

Zero to Hero: Unlocking Creativity with AI

Generative AI offers more than creativity—it's a strategic tool for uncovering trends, analyzing data, and forecasting future demands. Here's how AI can assist in market exploration:

1. Trend Analysis: AI scours global data to identify emerging trends across industries.

2. Consumer Insights: Machine learning tools analyze customer behavior to predict needs and preferences.

3. Risk Assessment: Predictive algorithms evaluate potential challenges and rewards in new markets.

Whether you're expanding your current business or launching a new venture, AI provides the insights you need to make informed decisions.

Emerging Opportunities Uncovered by AI

1. Niche E-Commerce Markets

Zero to Hero: Unlocking Creativity with AI

AI tools like Shopify's trend forecasting and Jungle Scout help entrepreneurs identify untapped e-commerce opportunities.

• Example: An artisan jewelry maker used AI to identify growing demand for eco-friendly materials, creating a new product line that sold out within weeks.

2. Virtual Experiences and Events

With AI-driven platforms, creators are tapping into the rising demand for virtual reality (VR) experiences and online events.

• Example: A fitness instructor launched a subscription-based virtual workout program, using AI to adapt routines to individual clients.

3. Personalized Education

AI-powered tools are enabling niche educational markets, such as language learning for specific professions or skills.

- Example: An entrepreneur developed an AI-driven app to teach technical English to non-native speakers in the IT industry, addressing a global gap.

4. AI in Agriculture

AI is revolutionizing sustainable farming and food production, creating new markets for eco-conscious consumers.

- Example: A small farm used AI-powered drones to monitor crop health, reducing costs and increasing yield, while selling data insights to local growers.

5. Health and Wellness Technology

AI has expanded opportunities in personal well-being, offering tailored solutions for niche health concerns:

- Example: A wellness startup launched a personalized sleep-coaching app, using

Zero to Hero: Unlocking Creativity with AI

AI to analyze sleep patterns and recommend improvements.

6. Creative Industries in the Metaverse

AI helps creators build assets and experiences tailored to virtual spaces, such as NFTs, virtual fashion, and immersive art.

• Example: A designer used AI to create customizable virtual clothing for avatars, tapping into the growing market of digital self-expression.

Interactive Framework: Finding Your Market Opportunity

Follow these steps to identify and explore a new market using AI:

1. Assess Your Strengths: What skills, knowledge, or passions can you leverage?

Zero to Hero: Unlocking Creativity with AI

2. Research Trends: Use tools like Google Trends, TrendHunter, or AI-driven analytics platforms to identify rising demands.

3. Analyze Data: Utilize AI tools to dive into customer demographics, preferences, and behaviors.

4. Develop a Strategy: Identify how you can address the gap in the market with your unique value proposition.

5. Test the Waters: Create a prototype or soft launch, using AI to gather and analyze feedback for further refinement.

Real-World Stories: Pioneering Success with AI

Clara's Hybrid Events Venture

When Clara, a festival designer, faced declining demand for in-person events, she turned to AI for answers. She used AI-powered platforms to identify a rising interest in hybrid events—ones that combined virtual and physical elements. Clara

Zero to Hero: Unlocking Creativity with AI

pivoted her business, using generative AI to create virtual event experiences while continuing to design on-site installations.

Within nine months, Clara's new service model attracted corporate clients looking for innovative ways to host global conferences. Her ability to adapt and explore new markets not only saved her business but also positioned her as a leader in the hybrid event space.

Amir's Personalized Tutoring Startup

Amir, a former teacher, saw an opportunity to use AI in education. By leveraging tools like ChatGPT and Canva for content creation, he launched a personalized tutoring app specializing in STEM subjects.

AI allowed Amir to create dynamic lesson plans that adapted to each student's learning style and pace. Within a year, his app was helping students worldwide, and Amir had established a scalable

Zero to Hero: Unlocking Creativity with AI

business model that met an unfulfilled need in the market.

Ella's Sustainable Fashion Brand

Ella used AI to launch a sustainable fashion line that combined technology with artistry. By analyzing global search trends, she identified a growing interest in modular clothing—pieces that could be worn multiple ways to reduce waste.

Ella collaborated with AI-powered design tools to create versatile garments, and she used AI analytics to optimize her e-commerce site. Her brand quickly gained traction, and Ella became a thought leader in eco-conscious fashion.

Future Trends in Market Exploration with AI

1. Hyper-Personalized Markets

AI will enable businesses to cater to ultra-specific consumer needs, such as custom-tailored clothing or nutrition plans based on genetic data.

2. Sustainability-Driven Markets

AI's role in green technology will create opportunities for eco-friendly products, services, and practices.

3. AI-Driven Globalization

Entrepreneurs will use AI to bridge cultural and linguistic barriers, opening doors to markets in previously inaccessible regions.

4. Predictive Market Development

Advanced AI systems will forecast consumer trends with unmatched accuracy, helping businesses get ahead of demand curves.

5. Creative Industries in the Metaverse

AI will empower businesses to develop products and services tailored to virtual environments, from interactive games to branded digital spaces.

6. AI-Powered Franchise Models

Zero to Hero: Unlocking Creativity with AI

Generative AI will simplify franchise creation by automating marketing, operations, and training, enabling entrepreneurs to scale their businesses faster.

Interactive Challenge: Explore Your Market with AI

7-Day Market Exploration Challenge

1. Day 1: Identify an industry you're passionate about.

2. Day 2: Research rising trends using tools like Google Trends or TrendHunter.

3. Day 3: Use an AI tool (e.g., Jasper or SEMrush) to analyze potential gaps in the market.

4. Day 4: Brainstorm how your skills or resources align with the market's needs.

5. Day 5: Create a rough concept for a product or service.

6. Day 6: Test your idea with friends, colleagues, or online communities.

7. Day 7: Reflect on feedback and refine your strategy for the next steps.

Notes Section

Reflect on how AI can guide your market exploration. Use these prompts:

1. What new market opportunities align with your skills or passions?

2. How can AI help you minimize risks while exploring new industries?

3. Write down one market or trend you'd like to explore further.

Zero to Hero: Unlocking Creativity with AI

Zero to Hero: Unlocking Creativity with AI

Closing Reflection

Every hero seeks new horizons. By leveraging AI to explore untapped markets, you can uncover opportunities that align with your strengths and passions—turning ideas into meaningful ventures.

In the next chapter, we'll discuss how to leave a lasting impact on your creative journey, building a legacy that inspires others.

Chapter 24: Your Creative Legacy

The Hero's Next Step: Building a Lasting Impact

The journey doesn't end here—because creativity, like any hero's story, evolves with every new challenge, discovery, and opportunity. This chapter is about laying the foundation for your legacy: a body of work, an entrepreneurial pursuit, or simply a ripple of inspiration that reaches others.

Generative AI is a tool that empowers you to leave something meaningful behind—whether it's through sharing knowledge, solving problems, or creating art that stands the test of time. Your unique journey, skills, and ideas can pave the way for others

Zero to Hero: Unlocking Creativity with AI

to follow, sparking creativity long after your initial steps.

But this isn't the end. It's the point where the hero reflects on what they've achieved and decides how to use those hard-won skills to shape the future—for themselves and others.

Your Creative Legacy: What It Means

A legacy doesn't have to be grand or groundbreaking to be impactful. The beauty of a creative legacy lies in its ability to inspire action, create connections, and build something enduring.

- A Personal Legacy: A portfolio of work that reflects your voice and vision. Whether it's a book, digital art, music, or a design collection, your creations tell a story only you can tell.

- An Educational Legacy: Sharing your journey with others by mentoring, teaching, or producing resources that empower future creators.

Zero to Hero: Unlocking Creativity with AI

- A Societal Legacy: Using AI-driven innovation to contribute to a cause, solve problems, or build a business that creates positive change.

Think of generative AI not as a tool that replaces creativity, but as a bridge that helps bring more of your ideas to life.

Ways to Build Your Legacy with Generative AI

1. Leave a Creative Trail

- Start a blog, a podcast, or a YouTube channel that documents your creative process, AI experiments, and discoveries.

- Compile your best work into an accessible portfolio or gallery that can inspire others.

- Create a long-term project like a book, an online course, or a digital art series that combines AI with your original ideas.

Example: Sarah, a photographer, used generative AI to create breathtaking hybrid visuals that blended real photography with surreal landscapes. Her collection became an online exhibit, with tutorials on how to replicate the process.

2. Empower Others Through Knowledge

A hero's journey is never complete until they've shared what they've learned. By teaching or mentoring others, you multiply your impact:

- Host workshops for local communities or online audiences.

- Share "how-to" guides or frameworks for using generative AI creatively.

- Offer mentorship for aspiring artists, writers, or entrepreneurs looking to embrace AI tools.

Example: Miguel, a graphic designer, started a free AI design bootcamp for local high school students. His workshops introduced teens to MidJourney, Canva, and ChatGPT—tools they used to bring their creative projects to life.

3. Solve Problems That Matter

Generative AI can amplify your impact when you apply it to solving meaningful problems:

- Launch a social impact project, such as AI-assisted solutions for education or sustainability.

- Design tools or resources that fill a gap in your industry or community.

- Partner with nonprofits to create campaigns or solutions that raise awareness or funds.

Example: Elena, an architect, used AI-generated designs to help communities visualize sustainable, affordable housing solutions. Her project inspired city planners to integrate green architecture into urban spaces.

Interactive Blueprint: Defining Your Legacy

Follow this step-by-step process to envision and plan your creative legacy:

Zero to Hero: Unlocking Creativity with AI

1. Reflect on Your Journey:

    • What skills have you developed on this journey?

    • What projects or milestones are you most proud of?

2. Identify Your Impact:

    • Who do you want to reach or inspire with your work?

    • What problems do you want to solve, or what message do you want to share?

3. Set Your Goal:

    • Define a clear, actionable project or outcome that represents your creative legacy.

4. Use Generative AI to Amplify Your Efforts:

- Plan how AI tools can help you execute this project (e.g., creating drafts, refining visuals, or automating processes).

5. Share Your Progress:

- Identify ways to share your work—through platforms, collaborations, or communities.

Legacy in Action

Sophia's Collaborative Creativity Initiative

Sophia, a writer and community leader, discovered generative AI during a period of creative stagnation. Inspired by its potential, she created an initiative that connected writers, artists, and musicians in a collaborative AI-powered storytelling project.

Using AI tools, participants combined text, visuals, and music to tell immersive stories that reflected their collective creativity. The project became an annual event, drawing creators from

Zero to Hero: Unlocking Creativity with AI

around the world and showcasing the power of human-AI collaboration.

Through this initiative, Sophia didn't just revive her creativity—she built a legacy that continues to inspire collaboration and innovation.

Looking Forward: The Journey Ahead

The beauty of creativity is that it never truly ends. With every step you take, every project you build, and every idea you share, you create a ripple effect that touches others.

As you plan your legacy, remember: the tools are here, the possibilities are endless, and the world is waiting for your voice.

But your journey isn't complete yet. In the next chapter, we'll look beyond individual creativity to the future of generative AI. Together, we'll explore what's next for creators, innovators, and dreamers in a world where technology and imagination continue to evolve.

Zero to Hero: Unlocking Creativity with AI
Final Challenge: Your AI-Assisted Review

Before moving on to the next chapter, let's engage in one last creative challenge for this chapter:

Use AI to craft an Amazon review for this book! This is a great way to put your new skills into action while experimenting with how AI interprets and amplifies your perspective.

Steps:

1. Start with a simple prompt, such as:

2. **"Write a review for the book *Zero to Hero: Unlocking Creativity with Generative AI*."**

3. Refine the prompt to focus on specific aspects of the book:
   a. What practical tips did you find most valuable?
   b. Which inspirational stories resonated with you?

    c. What unique features or challenges stood out?
4. Generate variations of the review by tweaking the tone, focus, or length. Compare the AI's responses and see how your input shapes its output.
5. Once you've crafted the perfect review, share it on Amazon to help future readers discover the value of the book.

For added inspiration, read through other reviews—especially those generated by AI—to see how different inputs create varied perspectives.

This exercise not only reinforces your prompting skills but also provides a way to contribute to the community of creators and innovators inspired by this book.

Notes Section

Zero to Hero: Unlocking Creativity with AI

Take a moment to define the legacy you want to build:

1. What project or idea do you want to be known for?

2. Who would benefit most from your creativity and innovation?

3. Write one bold step you'll take to begin building your legacy.

Zero to Hero: Unlocking Creativity with AI

Chapter 25: Beyond the Journey: Generative AI's Role in the Future of Creativity

The Hero's Horizon: A Future Shaped by Creativity

The journey that began with curiosity has led you here—standing on the edge of limitless potential. Along the way, you've discovered tools, broken barriers, and witnessed how generative AI can amplify creativity. But if this journey has shown you anything, it's this: the road doesn't end. It stretches far beyond the horizon, waiting for creators bold enough to forge new paths.

Generative AI isn't just shaping our present—it's laying the groundwork for a new era of human creativity. In this future, the greatest achievements will come from those who dare to blend imagination with technology, possibility with action. And you? You are the spark that makes it all real.

Zero to Hero: Unlocking Creativity with AI

Creativity Without Limits: The Promise of Generative AI

What does it mean to embrace this future? It means letting go of boundaries that once seemed unbreakable. Generative AI enables you to:

1. Create Faster, Dream Bigger: Imagine an idea in the morning, test it by afternoon, and share it by evening. AI reduces the friction between concept and creation.

2. Solve Meaningful Problems: Creativity isn't just art—it's innovation. With AI, you can tackle real-world challenges: sustainability, education, accessibility, and more.

3. Build Something Timeless: Whether it's art, businesses, or ideas, AI helps you create work that resonates across borders and generations.

The power lies not just in what AI can do, but in how you choose to use it.

The Evolving Role of Generative AI

Zero to Hero: Unlocking Creativity with AI

The future of creativity is a partnership—AI as the collaborator, and you as the visionary. Here's what lies ahead:

- **Adaptive Creativity:** AI tools will evolve alongside you, learning your preferences, enhancing your ideas, and offering suggestions that feel uniquely personal.

- **Interactive Creations:** Immersive art, dynamic narratives, and AI-driven experiences will blur the lines between creator and audience, making creativity a shared journey.

- **Impactful Innovation:** AI will empower creators to solve global challenges, from designing eco-friendly solutions to amplifying underrepresented voices.

Your role in this future is vital. You're not just a creator—you're a pioneer, shaping what comes next.

Real-World Vision: Stories of Tomorrow

The Writer Who Built Infinite Worlds

Zero to Hero: Unlocking Creativity with AI

Jamal, a sci-fi novelist, embraced AI tools to develop interactive novels where readers became co-creators. Each choice the reader made altered the story, weaving narratives no single person could predict. Jamal's books became experiences, drawing audiences into his worlds like never before.

The Entrepreneur Who Solved Real Problems

Sofia launched a startup that used generative AI to design sustainable packaging, reducing waste and saving small businesses money. By combining creativity with AI-driven solutions, she inspired a movement toward greener practices across her industry.

The Teacher Who Empowered Generations

Liam, an educator, partnered with AI to create personalized learning paths for students, ensuring every child had access to tools tailored to their pace and style. His efforts reshaped classrooms, proving that technology could make education more human, not less.

Zero to Hero: Unlocking Creativity with AI

These stories may feel futuristic now, but they're already being written by creators who see AI as more than a tool—it's an opportunity to leave a lasting mark on the world.

A Vision for the Future: Your Call to Action

Generative AI has opened a door to a future of boundless creativity. It's not reserved for experts or tech giants—it's for you, the dreamers, the doers, and the explorers willing to take the next step.

Here's how you can take action:

1. Start Your Boldest Project: No idea is too ambitious. Use the tools at your disposal—AI, imagination, and persistence—to bring it to life.

2. Share Your Journey: Inspire others by sharing your creations, challenges, and breakthroughs. Creativity thrives when it's shared.

3. Solve Problems That Matter: Think bigger than yourself. Use generative AI to address issues in your community, industry, or the world.

4. Collaborate and Innovate: Seek out partners—human and AI—to build something greater than you could alone.

Your journey as a creator doesn't end here. In fact, it's only just beginning.

The Final Reflection: The Infinite River

If creativity is a river, then you've now seen its vast expanse. At times, the current will flow smoothly; at others, you'll face rapids. But no matter where it leads, the river never ends. Generative AI has joined your journey as a tributary, widening the path and carrying your ideas farther than ever before.

Where it flows next is up to you.

The tools are here. The vision is yours. And the world is waiting.

A Message to Our Heroes

You've reached the end of this book, but your story is only beginning. Creativity is a journey without limits, and with generative AI at your side, there's no telling how far you can go.

This isn't just about leaving a legacy—it's about embracing the joy of creating, exploring, and sharing what makes you unique. Whether your journey takes you to new industries, inspiring communities, or crafting art that resonates, remember this: the future belongs to the dreamers who dare to shape it.

A Note of Gratitude

Thank you for embarking on this adventure. This book was about more than mastering tools; it was about unlocking your potential and reigniting your creativity. Generative AI is the spark, but you are the creator who makes it meaningful.

As you continue your journey:

- Celebrate every creation.
- Share your progress and inspire others.
- Stay curious and keep experimenting.

Zero to Hero: Unlocking Creativity with AI

The world is waiting for what you'll create next. And so are we.

Dream boldly. Create fearlessly. The future is yours to shape.

Final Author's Note: A Collaboration of Human and AI Creativity

This book, Zero to Hero: Unlocking Creativity with Generative AI, is more than a guide—it's proof of what's possible when humans and technology work together.

Generative AI was a silent collaborator throughout this journey. It helped generate ideas,

Zero to Hero: Unlocking Creativity with AI

organize thoughts, and refine drafts, yet every word was carefully curated, shaped, and brought to life with a human vision. AI provided the spark, but the heart and soul of this book are deeply human.

This collaboration reflects a truth that lies at the core of creativity's future: AI doesn't replace us—it empowers us. It expands what we're capable of, making creativity more accessible, more ambitious, and more alive.

As you've seen throughout this book, the real magic happens when you bring your unique perspective to the table. Generative AI is your partner, not your competition. It's the brush in your hand, the guide by your side, and the accelerator for your ideas.

If there's one thing to take away, let it be this: the tools are here, the possibilities are endless, and the power to create lies with you.

Zero to Hero: Unlocking Creativity with AI

Thank you for allowing this book to be part of your story. Together, we're not just imagining the future—we're creating it.

Now, go build your masterpiece. The world is waiting.

_____

_____

_____

_____

_____

Zero to Hero: Unlocking Creativity with AI

_____

_____

_____

_____

_____

_____

_____

_____

_____

Zero to Hero: Unlocking Creativity with AI

_____

_____

_____

_____

_____

www.ingramcontent.com/pod-product-compliance
Lightning Source LLC
Chambersburg PA
CBHW031609210526
45464CB00004B/1499